Healing Hands

The Life and Legacy of Dr. Prakash Bangani

Preface

In the world of medicine and healing, there are the rare few whose impact extends far beyond the confines of their profession. Among these luminaries, Dr. Prakash Bangani shines with an extraordinary brilliance that touches every life he encounters. This book is a testament to his remarkable journey—a journey marked not only by medical expertise but also by a profound compassion that transcends the boundaries of conventional care.

Dr. Bangani's story is one of unwavering dedication and boundless empathy. He is a beacon of hope in a world often shadowed by adversity. His commitment to healing goes beyond the mere physical; he is a master of the delicate art of mending both body and soul. Each patient who crosses his path experiences more than just medical treatment—they encounter a gentle spirit who understands the deepest fears and struggles of the human condition.

As you turn the pages of this book, you will embark on a journey through the life of a man whose influence extends far beyond the sterile walls of a clinic. Whose acts of compassion ripple through the lives of the most vulnerable, bringing light where there was darkness and offering a future where there was once only despair.

Dr. Bangani's legacy is built on a foundation of selfless service and tireless commitment. His story is a testament to the profound impact that one person can have when driven by a genuine desire to make the world a better place. It is a reminder that true greatness lies not in the accolades we receive, but in the lives we touch and the hearts we heal.

In sharing the achievements, challenges, and transformative moments of Dr. Bangani's life, this book aims to honor his extraordinary contributions and inspire others to embrace a similar path of compassion and dedication. His journey is a guiding light for anyone who aspires to make a difference in the lives of others and to leave an indelible mark on the world.

The book is dedicated to the extraordinary life of Dr. Prakash Bangani—a true hero in the world of healing and a shining example of what it means to live a life devoted to the service of others.

The idea for this book was inspired by CA. Vipin Jain, Dr. Bangani's patient since 1994, who regards him as nothing less than a god. With this inspiration, Dr. Bangani's grandsons lent their support in bringing the book to life—and the rest, as they say, is history.

"The secret of living is giving"- Dr. Prakash Bangani

TABLE OF CONTENTS

1. Roots of Dedication — 03
2. Pursuit of Healing Wisdom — 07
3. Choosing Orthopedics: A Calling — 11
4. Credentials and Commitments — 19
5. An Empire Forms: Start of the Private Practice — 23
6. Turning a New Leaf — 29
7. Returning Home — 37
8. Challenges of Change — 43
9. Revolutionizing Orthopedics in Indore — 45
10. Transforming Practices — 49
11. Legacy of Excellence — 53
12. A Ray of Hope Amidst Darkness — 57
13. Orthopedic Pedagogy — 63
14. Mother: The Guiding Force — 69
15. Family as a Pillar — 71
16. Arihant Hospital & Research Centre — 77
17. Shri Jain Shwetambar Academy — 83
18. Temple of Service — 89
19. Impact Beyond Medicine — 93
20. Bhagwan Mahavir Viklang Sahayata Samiti — 97
21. Achievements, Leadership, and Lasting Impact — 103
22. Monk in the World of Orthopedics — 109

- **Conclusion** — 113
- **Messages from closed ones...........** — 115

Our Nana, Dr. Prakash Bangani, has lived a revolutionary and inspirational life, built upon unwavering purpose and commitment to humanity. Through his work as an orthopedic surgeon and his philanthropic efforts for over 50 years, he has directly and indirectly impacted the lives of countless individuals. With a firm resolve and intent to heal, our Nana has exemplified the highest degree of compassion and integrity for his patients, peers, friends, and family. In doing so, he has earned profound respect and adoration from people all around the world.

While Nana's professional and philanthropic achievements are impressive, it is his role as our grandfather that is most special. We are forever grateful for the moments and memories we have had the opportunity to share with Nana and Nani over the course of our lives. Whether it was picking mangoes off a tree, teaching us about Jainism on summer mornings in Indore, playing Canaasta with us at the dining table, or watching Wimbledon in July, Nana has always guided us with love, wisdom, and support. He has shown us what it means to live with compassion, integrity, and dedication to others. His life is a model we aspire to follow, and we are proud to carry on his legacy for generations to come.

We love you so much Nana! Thank you for showing us the way.

And to our Nani: there was no Nana without you. We love you and we miss you immensely!

With utmost love,
~Your grandchildren ~
Ankush, Kunaal, Aakash, Kurren, Milan, and Deeya

Early Life and Family

Roots of Dedication

Dr. Prakash Bangani was born on August 10, 1941, into a lower middle-class joint family hailing from Indore, Madhya Pradesh. His familial unit comprised his grandfather, father, mother, an elder brother (Shikhar Chand Nagori), an elder sister (Shanta Ben), and a younger sister (Chandan Bala), all devout adherents of the Jain faith.

Prakash's family roots trace back to Nagore, Rajasthan, with his grandfather, Ganesh Maldi Nagori, originally hailing from the region before relocating to Indore. His parents, Lal Chand Nagori and Panchi Bai Nagori, epitomized simplicity and humility, embodying the virtues of Jainism in their everyday lives. Despite their limited formal education, they possessed a remarkable intellect and unwavering devotion to their faith.

In the 1940s, Prakash's father, Lal Chand, found himself drawn to the world of gambling, (satta). However, a pivotal moment arrived when, upon the advice of a Jain saint, Lal Chand made the decision to retire from his work at the young age of 45. This transition marked a turning point in his life, guiding him towards a path of spiritual reflection and personal growth.

Meanwhile, Prakash's mother, a formidable and astute woman, played a pivotal role in managing their household and guiding the family's decisions. Her influence extended beyond the confines of their home, as she harbored a deep desire to contribute to the welfare of society. From Prakash's early years, both his parents endeavored to instill a strong sense of religious devotion in their children, nurturing their spiritual growth and fostering a deep connection to their Jain heritage.

From his earliest days, young Prakash found himself immersed in the teachings and traditions of his family's religion, although his inquisitive mind often sought more tangible experiences.

His family ran a shop in the cloth market area, with his father serving as a wholesale merchant, while his mother managed the household affairs as a homemaker. Prakash's parents, devout practitioners of Jainism, remained steadfast in their efforts to cultivate religious devotion in their children. Through daily rituals and teachings, they sought to instill a deep-rooted appreciation for their faith in the young minds under their care.

Despite his parents' earnest efforts to impart religious values, Prakash's interests veered toward the practical aspects of life. His daily routine included his mother's insistence on temple visits and prayers, a task met with reluctance by the young boy. However, the consequences of defying his mother's wishes were clear: no milk, a precious commodity for the milk-loving child.

One day, in a bid to reconcile his desire for milk with his aversion to temple visits, Prakash devised a cunning plan. Driven by the mischievous workings of a child's mind, Prakash decided to outwit his mother's expectations. With a twinkle in his eye and a plan forming in his playful imagination, he stealthily slipped out of the house, his heart racing with excitement. Briefly lingering outside, he savored the thrill of his adventure before returning home, ready to share his tale of religious devotion. Yet, despite his best efforts to mask his true intentions, his mother's innate intuition proved to be a formidable adversary. Undeterred by initial setbacks, Prakash persisted in his playful antics, determined to outsmart his mother. But when he realized he had forgotten to put tilak on his forehead, his mischievous plans were exposed, and he missed out on his beloved milk.

Though his parents lacked formal education, Prakash emerged as a mischievous yet brilliant child from the very beginning. His insatiable curiosity led him on a constant quest for new discoveries and adventures.

Growing up in an era devoid of private schooling, Prakash received his education from a public school nestled behind Bada Sarafa. At just six years old, he embarked on his academic journey, swiftly excelling and consistently ranking at the top of his class. However, he continued his mischiefs, and engaged in playful antics with his friends, particularly relishing the moments after school.

Throughout his primary years, Prakash's exceptional intellect earned him early promotions from second to third grade, showcasing his innate brilliance. Yet, as he entered middle school, his vibrant social circle often led him astray, indulging in various extracurricular escapades. However, these adventures came at a cost, as Prakash found himself facing a setback with a supplementary exam in the eighth grade after failing his first attempt.

Ironically, this stumble proved to be a turning point in Prakash's journey. Recognizing the need for greater discipline and dedication, he resolved to excel, driven by his aspiration to become a doctor. Two years later, in the tenth grade, his determination bore fruit as he not only passed but scored the top position in his class, signaling the beginning of his remarkable academic trajectory.

02

Pursuit of Healing Wisdom

At 9 years old, Prakash went through a very difficult experience when his older brother, Shikhar Chand Nagori, fell gravely ill with severe pneumonia. In an era where medical resources were scarce, especially for common folk, pneumonia posed a significant threat due to the limited availability of treatment options. At that critical juncture, penicillin, the first antibiotic introduced in India, had just emerged but was not easily accessible.

Indore's senior doctors painted a bleak picture, declaring that Shikhar's chances of survival were slim. However, their family doctor, a beacon of hope amidst despair, urged them to give treatment a chance. Despite facing numerous hurdles, including the challenge of maintaining the required chilling temperature for the penicillin, which their family lacked due to the absence of a refrigerator, they persevered.

Fortunately, upon learning the gravity of the situation, their neighbor offered the use of their fridge to store the lifesaving medicine. With the doctor administering the penicillin four times a day and closely monitoring Shikhar's condition, a glimmer of hope emerged amidst the darkness of despair. Through a combination of divine intervention and the doctor's unwavering determination, Shikhar's life was miraculously spared.

This pivotal moment not only granted Shikhar a new lease on life but also catalyzed a profound transformation in Prakash's own destiny. It was on that fateful day that Prakash resolved to become a doctor himself, inspired by the miraculous intervention that had saved his brother's life.

Prakash stood at the edge of a transformative healing journey after graduating. However, life had a curveball in store for him, presented in the form of familial opposition. His aspiration was crystal clear—to pursue a career in biology and ultimately in Medicine. Yet, his parents vehemently opposed this choice. They cited ethical concerns about animal dissection. They viewed it as a moral transgression.

Compelled by parental authority, Prakash acquiesced to studying Commerce, albeit begrudgingly. Despite his excellent performance in his final exams, his heart was set on becoming a doctor. He expressed disillusionment with Commerce to his family and declared his unwillingness to continue down that path. Frustrations mounted as he adamantly voiced his desire to delve into biology and chemistry instead. In a pivotal moment, his mother devised a compromise. Prakash would assist in managing the family business alongside his father. However, his elder siblings intervened. They advocated passionately for Prakash's dream of becoming a doctor. They argued persuasively that, as a physician, he could positively impact their community and enhance lives.

After extensive deliberation and impassioned exchanges, his parents relented, granting Prakash the long-awaited permission to pursue his dream of studying medicine. And so, with unwavering determination, Prakash embarked on his journey through medical school, poised to make a profound difference in the lives of others.

Prakash with his wife Saroj, Elder brother Shikhar Chand Nagori, and sister Shantaben

Growing up in an era devoid of private schooling, Prakash received his education from a public school nestled behind Bada Sarafa. At just six years old, he embarked on his academic journey, swiftly excelling and consistently ranking at the top of his class. However, he continued his mischiefs, and engaged in playful antics with his friends, particularly relishing the moments after school.

Throughout his primary years, Prakash's exceptional intellect earned him early promotions from second to third grade, showcasing his innate brilliance. Yet, as he entered middle school, his vibrant social circle often led him astray, indulging in various extracurricular escapades. However, these adventures came at a cost, as Prakash found himself facing a setback with a supplementary exam in the eighth grade after failing his first attempt.

Ironically, this stumble proved to be a turning point in Prakash's journey. Recognizing the need for greater discipline and dedication, he resolved to excel, driven by his aspiration to become a doctor. Two years later, in the tenth grade, his determination bore fruit as he not only passed but scored the top position in his class, signaling the beginning of his remarkable academic trajectory.

03

Choosing Orthopedics: A Calling

After completing a two-year internship, Prakash embarked on his pre-medical college journey in 1958. Upon entering his classes, he noticed a plethora of students sharing his surname, Jain. Eager to carve out his own distinct identity, he made the bold decision to seek a legal change of his last name from Jain to Bangani.

In those days, securing admission to a preferred medical school hinged greatly on one's performance in the pre-med college exam. Naturally, Prakash excelled with distinction, earning himself a coveted spot at Indore Medical College, a program spanning five rigorous years. Throughout his tenure, he devoted himself to his studies while also assuming leadership roles within his class. He served as the monitor and later as the President during both his 1st and 3rd years, overseeing the academic affairs with diligence. Additionally, he took on the responsibility of class secretary in his second year, demonstrating his commitment to academic and administrative excellence. Not limiting himself to the confines of academia, Prakash also showcased his talents on the cricket field, representing his college with pride.

Driven by a steadfast determination to pursue surgery, Prakash set his sights on achieving top honors in the final exam. In those days, only the top four students in the class were granted the esteemed opportunity to specialize in surgery. Despite his resolute focus, a significant development altered Prakash's trajectory.

In December 1963, during his third year of medical college, Prakash was engaged to Saroj, with the understanding that they would postpone their nuptials until after his graduation. However, unforeseen circumstances led to a change in plans, with his in-laws persuading Prakash's mother to advance the wedding date, allowing them to marry four months before the final MD exam. This decision left Prakash in a state of apprehension, as he grappled with the daunting task of maintaining his academic aspirations alongside his new marital responsibilities. Determined to excel despite the challenges, Prakash made the difficult choice to separate from his wife temporarily, urging her to reside with his parents for the time being, while he dedicated himself to intensive study. Seeking complete isolation from external distractions, he relocated to a hostel for the four-month period leading up to the exam.

Despite his meticulous preparation and consistent academic performance, fate dealt Prakash a slight setback when he placed fifth in the final exam, just one position shy of securing a spot in surgery. However, fortune smiled upon him when the student who topped the class expressed a preference for pediatrics over surgery. Seizing this unexpected opportunity, Prakash found himself on the path to surgical specialization at Indore hospital, a testament to his unwavering determination and resilience in the face of adversity.

Once he embarked on his surgical journey, life took a decisive turn. The realm of theory gave way to the practical realm, marking the beginning of hands-on experience. Pursuing his MS in General Surgery, Dr. Prakash found himself under the guidance of the esteemed Dr. Chamanlal during his formative years. Dr. Chamanlal, renowned for his clinical prowess and teaching acumen, particularly in cardiac surgery, took Prakash under his wing. On Prakash's first day, Dr. Chamanlal delved into his house job experience, initiating a mentorship that involved Prakash in numerous surgical procedures to hone his skills. As they treated patients, Dr. Chamanlal assumed the role of assistant while Prakash took the lead. Tragically, Dr. Chamanlal's sudden demise due to a heart attack after a year and a half placed Dr. Agarwal, a prominent figure in the medical community at the time, in the role of Prakash's mentor.

At that time, there was one pivotal incident that reshaped Prakash's outlook on life as a doctor. During his younger sister's wedding. While on vacation, communal riots erupted in the city, flooding hospitals with patients in need of urgent care. Prakash was swiftly summoned back to work, abruptly departing from the celebratory atmosphere at home. This experience left an indelible impression on him, instilling values of discipline, dedication to duty, and the profound responsibilities borne by a true physician.

As days turned into months and months into years, Dr. Prakash persisted on his journey, eventually completing his MS degree in General Surgery in 1964.

In 1966, an encounter with Dr. Bandi, an American-trained educator, marked a turning point for Prakash's ambitions. Having harbored a desire to pursue cardiac surgery in the United States since his medical school days, Prakash seized the opportunity to discuss this aspiration with Dr. Bandi. The conversation turned to the necessary requirements for studying in America, including the ECFMG exam, which Prakash had already cleared during his fourth year of medical school.

During their conversation, Dr. Bandi posed a crucial question: would Prakash commit to government service upon returning from the United States? Prakash's negative response prompted Dr. Bandi to advise him to forgo pursuing his MS Post Grad in General Surgery in India and instead head to America immediately. This advice left Prakash torn between his instincts to embark on his American journey and the rational choice to complete his studies in India.

Seeking counsel, Prakash consulted with three colleagues, who viewed his inclination towards America with skepticism. Despite their reservations, Prakash ultimately followed his heart and decided to pursue his American dream, notwithstanding his friends' dissent.

With his sights set on working in America, Prakash embarked on the arduous process of applying for residencies. Dr. Bandi's guidance led him to the library, where he perused a green book containing detailed information about American universities. Spending five hours meticulously selecting six hospitals offering the highest pay, Prakash presented his choices to Dr. Bandi. However, Dr. Bandi's response was unexpected; he questioned Prakash's aspirations, likening his choices to those of a racehorse versus a donkey. Redirecting Prakash's focus, Dr. Bandi emphasized the importance of prioritizing universities with public hospitals, despite the lower salaries they offered. While this adjustment required Prakash to lower his initial standards, it increased his chances of admission as an international student—a significant hurdle in his pursuit of practicing medicine in the United States.

Armed with Dr. Bandi's advice, Prakash revised his approach, applying to a targeted list of public schools with reputable hospital affiliations. He awaited eagerly for responses regarding his admission, knowing that securing a spot would be the first step towards realizing his American dream.

Many hospitals mandated a 6-month internship in general surgery before admitting candidates to their residency programs. To streamline his application process, Prakash had to correspond with these hospitals, explaining that his extensive three years of prior experience in general surgery rendered the internship redundant. Initially regarded as a potential intern by many hospitals, Prakash received favorable responses from the University of Pittsburgh and the University of Florida, both of which waived his internship requirement. Facing a choice between the two institutions, Prakash sought guidance from Dr. Bandi, who recommended the University of Pittsburgh.

In 1967, Prakash set out for America, embarking on his journey to Pittsburgh alone. Opting for a detour through the Pacific, Prakash planned stops in Japan, Hawaii, and several iconic American cities en route to Pittsburgh. Prior to departure, he sought counsel from Shikhar Chand (Jeesa) and was directed to a friend in Bangkok who offered financial assistance.

Arriving in Bangkok, Prakash borrowed $100 before proceeding to Japan to spend a week with Jeesa in Osaka. Additional funds were loaned from Jeesa before Prakash continued his journey to Honolulu, where he encountered culinary challenges as a vegetarian. In San Francisco, Los Angeles, and Las Vegas, Prakash marveled at the sights and experiences, including Hollywood, Disneyland, and the novelty of vast shopping malls.

Despite a setback in Las Vegas, where he lost $40 on a slot machine, leaving him with only $30 for further travel, Prakash persevered, finally reaching Pittsburgh after a brief stopover in New York City. Upon arrival, the University of Pittsburgh provided him with accommodation, but Prakash had to cover his other expenses. In a pinch, he sought financial assistance from the chief resident, securing a $50 loan to cover immediate needs.

Driven by his lifelong ambition to become a cardiac surgeon, Prakash sought guidance from Dr. Lal at UPMC. Despite warnings of the daunting challenges ahead, including a rigorous 7-year residency program, Prakash remained resolute in his determination to pursue this path. Securing a one-month posting through Dr. Lal, Prakash embarked on a demanding schedule, on call 24/7 and tasked with mastering the intricacies of the chief surgeon's patients—a crucial step toward realizing his dream.

Successfully completing his one-month stint under the guidance of Dr. Wilson, the chief surgeon, Prakash found himself in a pivotal interview where Dr. Wilson delved into his aspirations. Candidly expressing his desire to specialize in cardiac surgery, Prakash faced a difficult decision when Dr. Wilson extended an offer for a seven-year residency in cardiac surgery. Despite the tempting opportunity, Prakash grappled with his initial intention of working briefly in America before returning to India, compounded by the realization that the hospitals in India, specifically in Indore (his hometown) lacked an ICU, hindering his ability to practice upon his return. After careful deliberation, Prakash made the tough choice to decline the offer, setting his sights on exploring other avenues.

Prakash turned his attention to neurosurgery and secured an opportunity to shadow the chief surgeon for a month. However, a tragic turn during a surgery involving a brain aneurysm left Prakash deeply unsettled, signaling that neurosurgery might not align with his calling.

Redirecting his focus, Prakash turned to orthopedics, recognizing its broad market potential and comparatively lower fatality rates. Together with his wife, he diligently reached out to numerous hospitals, penning over 40 letters in pursuit of a residency. After three months of waiting, Prakash received responses from the University of Massachusetts and the University of Florida. Opting for the University of Massachusetts, Prakash commenced his three-year orthopedic residency, setting the stage for the next chapter of his medical journey.

Professional Ascension

04

Credentials and Commitments

During his residency, Prakash found himself under the wing of Dr. Eddie, a chief resident known for his kindness. Eddie believed in giving his residents opportunities to spread their wings, so when conferences in various cities came up, he made sure his team got the chance to attend. For Prakash, this meant he got to explore new places and meet different people, broadening his horizons along the way.

As Prakash neared the end of his residency, he knew he wanted to specialize in hand surgery. The dream seemed within reach when he discovered there were only four places offering hand surgery fellowships: Los Angeles, New York, Louisville, and New Orleans. Among them, Louisville held a special allure for Prakash. Excitedly, he applied for the fellowship in Louisville, hoping for the chance to hone his skills in hand surgery. But when the interview day arrived, Prakash was taken aback. In the interview, the questions focused everywhere but on his professional background, leaving him feeling disheartened as he left the interview room.

Back in Massachusetts, Prakash couldn't shake off the disappointment. But just when he thought all hope was lost, Eddie delivered the news he'd been waiting for: Prakash had been accepted for the fellowship in Louisville. It was a moment of pure joy and relief, marking the beginning of a new chapter in Prakash's journey as a hand surgeon.

In Louisville, Prakash found himself immersed in a whirlwind of learning and hard work. Despite earning a meager $250 each month and enduring grueling hours from dawn till late into the night, Prakash saw every moment as an opportunity to grow. Hand surgery became his obsession, and with each passing day, he absorbed knowledge like a sponge, honing his skills until they gleamed with confidence.

Dr. Prakash with his colleagues in USA

Meanwhile, back home, Saroj was carrying their third child and his two daughters Sangita and Anita held down the fort. Then came the day when Saroj's labor pains began. Prakash, torn between his duties at work and his responsibilities as a husband and soon-to-be father, made the frantic dash to the hospital, leaving his work behind. Three hours later, as he grappled with the conflicting demands of his personal and professional life, Dr. Kleinert intervened.

With a gentle yet firm hand, Dr. Kleinert reminded Prakash of what truly mattered. Family, he said, should always come first. Moved by Dr. Kleinert's wisdom and compassion, Prakash raced back to the hospital, heart pounding with anticipation.

And there, amidst the whirlwind of emotions, Prakash found a beautiful bouquet of flowers waiting for Saroj, a token of support and understanding from his mentor. In that moment, surrounded by love and warmth, Prakash knew he was exactly where he needed to be: by Saroj's side, ready to embrace the new chapter of their lives together.

As the months flew by, Prakash found himself nearing the end of his residency, with his sights set on returning to India alongside Saroj. The anticipation of their long-awaited homecoming filled them both with excitement and hope. Throughout Prakash's fellowship in Louisville, they had diligently saved up their earnings, around $5,000, eagerly looking forward to starting afresh in their homeland.

But just when they thought their dreams were within reach, fate dealt them a cruel blow. The bank where they had entrusted their hard-earned savings suddenly collapsed, leaving them in a state of disbelief and vulnerability. The financial security they had painstakingly built over the past five years crumbled before their eyes, leaving them adrift in uncertainty. Their plans to return to India now seemed like a distant dream, overshadowed by the harsh reality of their financial setback. With their cherished goal slipping further out of reach, Prakash and Saroj found themselves grappling with a future they had not prepared for, uncertain of what lay ahead.

Prakash cast his net wide in his search for employment, exploring various opportunities until he stumbled upon Charleston, WV—a place that immediately captured his heart. There, he found a job offering $30,000 per year, and the sense of security it provided made him feel like the wealthiest man alive. His new workplace was a bustling private practice, led by a seasoned doctor whose reputation preceded him. With over 30 years of success under its belt, the practice was perpetually bustling with activity. Prakash and another American colleague dove headfirst into their roles, clocking in from the crack of dawn until the late hours of the night. Their schedule was relentless, with alternate nights spent on call, but the opportunity to contribute to such a dynamic environment filled Prakash with a sense of purpose and determination.

After eight months of hard work, Prakash made a shocking discovery that left him outraged. Despite personally generating an impressive $50,000 worth of business each month for the practice, his earnings amounted to a mere $2,500. It was a clear indication that the bulk of the profits were funneling directly into the owner's pockets, leaving Prakash feeling exploited and undervalued.

Fueled by a sense of injustice, Prakash wasted no time in confronting the head of the practice. With resolve in his voice, he announced his decision to quit come the first of January. However, his resignation was met with a desperate counteroffer from the owner: a staggering $100,000 per year. But Prakash remained steadfast in his principles. He understood the unique position he held as the sole hand surgeon in town and recognized the potential to earn far more than what was being offered. With confidence in his abilities and a determination to chart his own path, Prakash declined the lucrative offer, ready to seek out new opportunities that would allow him to thrive on his own terms.

05

An Empire Forms:
Start of the Private Practice

Dr. Prakash and his colleague, Dr. Ghiz, embarked on a bold journey in 1973, pooling their resources to establish a private practice in Charleston. With a mere $500 each in their bank accounts and no existing line of credit, they faced the daunting task of financing their venture. Undeterred by the financial challenge, they leveraged their status as physicians, instilling confidence in a hesitant bank to grant them a $100,000 loan.

Despite the pressing need to set up their practice, Dr. Prakash made the unconventional decision to take a trip to India, leaving Dr. Ghiz to handle the crucial setup alone. While his departure may have raised eyebrows, Dr. Prakash's unwavering trust in his partner's capabilities underscored their strong bond and shared vision for their future success.

But the road to success proved to be far rockier than they had anticipated. Despite their relentless dedication and tireless work ethic, financial prosperity remained elusive. They toiled day and night, yet the money trickled in at a painfully slow pace. Struggling to generate revenue, they found themselves in dire financial straits, unable to afford salaries for their employees or cover the practice's expenses. The once-promising venture now teetered on the brink of failure, testing the resolve and resilience of the two physicians as they navigated the challenges of entrepreneurship.

As their financial woes deepened, Dr. Prakash found himself in dire circumstances, unable to afford even the most basic necessities like a simple packet of bread. It was the lowest point in his life, reminding him of the tough challenges they faced in keeping their practice going.

Dr. Prakash Bangani

The overwhelming pressure and uncertainty of the situation tested Dr. Prakash's resolve like never before pushing him to the brink of despair, with his dreams dangling by a thread.

But in the depths of adversity, hope flickered. Dr. Prakash turned to his trusted friends, rallying their support and scraping together every penny they could spare. With $5,000 in hand, a lifeline emerged, breathing new life into their faltering practice. With renewed determination, they pressed on. Six months of relentless perseverance yielded unimaginable results. Suddenly, the tides began to turn, and the practice blossomed with newfound prosperity.

Emboldened by their success, Dr. Prakash took bold steps to secure their financial future. Establishing a profit-sharing pension fund in the second year and delving into the complexities of the stock market in the third, he navigated the intricate world of investments with skill and foresight.

But it was in the fourth year that the true testament of trust and partnership emerged. Dr. Ghiz, recognizing Dr. Prakash's prowess in financial matters, entrusted him with managing his own investments. With unwavering faith, Dr. Ghiz awaited only a single annual statement, confident in his friend's ability to safeguard their shared wealth.

And so, against all odds, amidst the trials and tribulations of their journey, Dr. Prakash and Dr. Ghiz emerged not just as successful entrepreneurs, but as lifelong comrades, bound together by the triumph of perseverance and the promise of a brighter tomorrow.

As the orthopedic practice expanded to include seven surgeons, Dr. Prakash's financial acumen extended beyond medicine. Recognizing an opportunity to diversify their investments, Dr. Prakash and four close friends from Charleston decided to pool their resources and venture into real estate.

Together, they invested in various properties including commercial buildings, shopping malls, and apartment complexes.

These investments offered a promising avenue for long-term growth and financial stability. Dr. Prakash assumed the responsibility of managing these properties, leveraging his expertise to ensure their success.

Through prudent decision-making and strategic management, their real estate portfolio flourished, contributing significantly to their collective wealth. This collaborative effort not only strengthened their financial standing but also solidified their bonds of friendship and trust.

Overall, their foray into real estate served as a testament to the power of teamwork, foresight, and sound financial management in achieving lasting success.

Between 1973 and 1986, Dr. Prakash's journey through the world of finance was akin to a rollercoaster ride, marked by ups and downs, triumphs and challenges. Yet, amidst it all, his strategic financial acumen and a stroke of luck with favorable tax regulations paved the way for a remarkable success story.

It all began when Dr. Prakash, with a heart as generous as his ambition, made a significant investment of $1.2 million in a cancer center. But this wasn't just any investment—it was a charitable gift. By channeling his funds into this noble cause, Dr. Prakash found a way to not only support a vital institution but also to navigate the labyrinth of tax regulations. The magic lay in the classification of his investment as a charitable contribution, a move that would prove to be a masterstroke in reducing his taxable income and, consequently, his tax liabilities.

As the years went by, Dr. Prakash's income soared, propelled by his dedication and hard work. Yet, despite the substantial increase in earnings, his tax burden seemed to lighten—a testament to the efficacy of his financial strategy.

But Dr. Prakash's journey wasn't solely defined by his charitable endeavors. A significant portion of his wealth found its home in the realm of real estate—a realm where savvy investors sought refuge for its tax advantages. Utilizing the declining balance method of depreciation over a 19-year period, Dr. Prakash deftly maneuvered through the intricacies of real estate investment, minimizing his tax obligations while maximizing his returns.

However, the winds of change were on the horizon. In 1986, President Reagan's Tax Reform Act shook the financial landscape to its core. Among its many provisions, the Act raised the capital gains tax rate, casting a shadow over the profitability of real estate investments. Moreover, changes to depreciation rules, including the transition to straight-line depreciation and extended depreciable life for properties, threatened to alter the equation for investors like Dr. Prakash.

Yet, through it all, Dr. Prakash remained undeterred. Armed with resilience and foresight, he adapted to the changing tides, navigating the complexities of the tax code with poise and precision. And though the road ahead might have been fraught with uncertainty, Dr. Prakash's story stood as a testament to the power of strategic planning, perseverance, and a touch of good fortune in the ever-evolving world of finance.

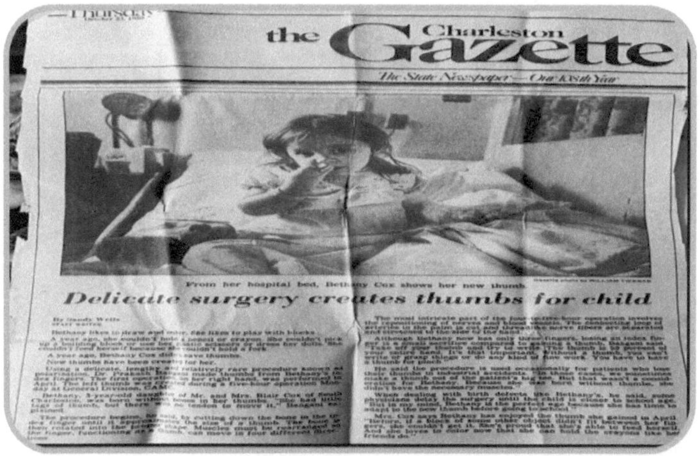

06

Turning a New Leaf

From 1973 to 1981, Dr. Prakash's life was a whirlwind of professional success and personal struggles, with the tug-of-war between duty and desire tugging at his heartstrings. Despite his accomplishments in America, a lingering sense of guilt gnawed at him—the feeling that he wasn't fulfilling his filial duties to care for his aging parents back in India.

In a bid to bridge the gap of distance and time, Prakash resolved to carve out a precious chunk of his busy schedule to reconnect with his roots. In 1981, he made a bold decision—to take a six-month hiatus from his bustling practice. His partner, Dr. Ghiz might have thought him crazy, but for Prakash, family came first.

With a heart brimming with anticipation and longing, Prakash extended an invitation to his parents—Dadasa and Dadisa—to join him in Palitana for a three-month sojourn. Knowing their reluctance to venture beyond the borders of India, he saw Palitana—a place deeply intertwined with his Jain heritage—as the perfect setting to reunite with his loved ones.

In the tranquil sanctity of Palitana, amidst the soft whispers of devotion and the lingering fragrance of incense, Prakash found himself drawn to the presence of a solitary monk—a figure of serene wisdom and gentle grace. Their daily rendezvous, a sacred hour shared from 4 to 5 pm, became a cherished ritual for Prakash, a time of reflection and connection that transcended the boundaries of time and space.

In the quiet solace of their encounters, Prakash poured out his heart to the monk, sharing his innermost thoughts, fears, and aspirations. And in return, the monk offered words of solace and wisdom, a beacon of light amidst the uncertainties of life. Each day, Prakash's mother urged the monk to convince him to return permanently to India, to which the monk always responded cryptically, "with time, everything will be alright."

Palitana Jain Temple

Palitana: A land with thousand temples on the hill

But it was on the eve of his departure, as the golden rays of dusk bathed Palitana in a warm embrace, that the monk sought a private audience with Prakash—a mere 15 minutes of his time, yet a moment that would alter the course of his destiny forever.

The monk posed a series of probing questions to Prakash. "How much do you spend per month in America?" he asked. Prakash, somewhat taken aback by the directness of the inquiry, confessed that his wife managed their expenses but offered an estimate nonetheless.

Undeterred, the monk delved deeper. "And how old are you?" he queried. Prakash, sensing the weight of the question, replied, "I am 41." The monk's next question hung in the air, heavy with significance. "Are you going to live 100 years?" he asked gently.

Prakash paused, his mind racing with possibilities. "Most likely not," he finally conceded. It was then that the monk imparted a series of insights that would forever alter Prakash's perspective on life and wealth.

With clarity born of years of contemplation, the monk outlined six essential units for a fulfilled life—a roadmap to financial security and personal fulfillment. From basic living expenses to provisions for his daughters' futures, from inflation to unforeseen medical expenses, each unit represented a cornerstone of a life well-lived.

Prakash listened intently, his heart stirred by the monk's wisdom. As they descended the steps of Palitana, the echoes of their conversation lingered in his mind. Returning to his wife, Saroj, Dr. Prakash shared the monk's teachings, and together they embarked on a journey of financial planning and introspection. They meticulously projected their expenses for the next 60 years, considering every aspect of their lives from basic necessities to unforeseen contingencies.

After much deliberation and careful calculation, they arrived at a figure that would ensure their security and enable them to live comfortably for the rest of their days.

$2 million—a sum that represented not just financial stability, but the realization of their dreams and aspirations.

In the year 1987, Dr. Prakash achieved a milestone that had long been the beacon guiding his aspirations—he amassed a wealth of $2 million. With this significant achievement, he made the resolute decision to return to his roots in India, to embrace a life imbued with the richness of his heritage and the warmth of familiar surroundings.

The months spent in Palitana were a blend of spiritual rejuvenation and familial bonding. Immersed in the peaceful atmosphere of the sacred city, Dr. Prakash found solace in the company of his parents, rekindling cherished memories and forging new connections. Yet, the toll of his self-imposed austerity was evident—so much so that even his own daughter, Sangita, failed to recognize the transformed figure standing before her at the airport upon his return.

But Dr. Prakash's quest for familial connection didn't end there. For the remaining three months of his sabbatical, he embarked on a grand odyssey across the length and breadth of India, accompanied by his three daughters and niece, Sunita. From the sun-kissed shores of South India to the misty landscapes of East India, from the bustling streets of West India to the serene valleys of Kashmir, their journey was a tapestry woven with threads of adventure, discovery, and familial love.

As they traveled the diverse landscapes and vibrant tapestries of India, Dr. Prakash reveled in the joy of experiencing his homeland through the eyes of his beloved daughters. Together, they created memories that would endure a lifetime, weaving a bond of love and kinship that transcended time and distance.

For Dr. Prakash, those six months were more than just a respite from his hectic life—they were a testament to the enduring power of family, the beauty of cultural heritage, and the indomitable spirit of a man driven by love and duty. And as he returned to his practice in America, his heart carried with it the echoes of laughter, the warmth of embraces, and the timeless treasures of a journey well-traveled.

Over the next six months, Prakash embarked on a journey of preparation, meticulously laying the groundwork for his return. Amidst the flurry of arrangements and logistics, one sentiment remained steadfast in his heart—a conviction that defied conventional wisdom.
With each passing day, as the moment of departure drew nearer, Prakash's heart swelled with anticipation and excitement. For him, the return to India was not just a physical journey, but a soulful homecoming—a reunion with the essence of his being and the fulfillment of a lifelong dream.

And as he embarked on this new chapter of his life, guided by the whims of his heart and the wisdom of his experiences, Dr. Prakash knew that he was stepping into a future filled with boundless possibilities and the promise of authentic fulfillment.

Evolution of an Orthopedic Surgeon

07

Returning Home

As the year 1988 dawned, Dr. Prakash found himself standing at a significant juncture in his life, grappling with the weight of decisions that would shape his future. For Dr. Prakash, the call of his homeland, India, resonated deeply within his soul, beckoning him back to the embrace of his roots.

With unwavering resolve, Dr. Prakash identified three compelling reasons that fueled his decision to embark on this transformative journey. Firstly, a sacred promise made to his beloved mother—a pledge to return and care for his aging parents, whose tender love and unwavering support had been the bedrock of his existence.

Secondly, driven by a profound sense of duty and community spirit, Dr. Prakash harbored a desire to continue practicing medicine, albeit on a part-time basis, in the bustling city of Indore. Here, amidst the vibrant tapestry of Indian life, he envisioned himself serving as a beacon of healing and hope, extending his expertise to uplift and empower those in need.

Yet, beyond the realms of duty and obligation, Dr. Prakash's heart yearned for a deeper connection—a spiritual pilgrimage of sorts. Rooted in the ancient traditions of Jainism, he sought to immerse himself in the rich tapestry of his religious heritage, delving deeper into its teachings and philosophies to nurture his soul and expand his spiritual horizons.

With these three pillars of purpose guiding his path, Dr. Prakash embarked on a journey of self-discovery and renewal, propelled by the timeless wisdom of his ancestors and the enduring bonds of love and devotion that bound him to his homeland.

Dr. Prakash with his wife Saroj and daughters-
Sangita, Anita, and Asha

With you, we built a home filled with love and
memories

And as he set forth on this sacred odyssey, he knew that every step taken was a testament to the enduring power of faith, family, and the indomitable spirit of the human heart. With anticipation and resolve, Dr. Prakash gathered his family— to share the momentous decision that had been weighing on his mind.

Dr. Prakash shared his plans to return to India, his homeland, where the echoes of his ancestry beckoned him back to the embrace of his roots. Yet, in a gesture of profound respect and love, he made it clear that the decision to accompany him rested solely with each member of his family—a choice to be made with their hearts and minds.

As the evening shadows lengthened, his eldest daughter, Sangita, with a quiet resolve shining in her eyes, expressed her desire to remain in the familiar embrace of America, to complete her studies in Boston University and pursue her dreams amidst the familiar landscapes of her youth. Dr. Prakash listened with a father's understanding, his heart swelling with pride at her determination and commitment.

On the other hand, Anita and Asha, the younger daughters of Dr. Prakash and Saroj, possessed a spirit unburdened by the weight of worldly concerns. With unwavering resolve and a sense of adventure, they made the courageous decision to embark on a journey back to India alongside their beloved parents, embracing a new chapter of life in the land of their ancestors. In the years preceding their departure, Dr. Prakash and Saroj took deliberate steps to ensure a smooth transition for their daughters. With tender affection and a silent promise of support, they bid farewell to Asha in 1984, followed by Anita in 1986, sending them ahead to India to pave the way for their family's reunion. It was a heartfelt gesture, born out of love and a desire to provide their daughters with a sense of comfort and familiarity as they embarked on this new adventure.

The departure of Anita and Asha marked the beginning of a new chapter for the Bangani family—one defined by resilience, unity, and resolute determination. With each passing day, their bond grew stronger, their spirits lifted by the promise of a new beginning.

And as they set foot on Indian soil once more, they did so with hearts full of hope and gratitude, ready to embrace the journey that lay ahead.

Afterwards, Dr. Prakash set out to untangle himself from the trappings of his life in America. He meticulously assessed his assets, recognizing that certain properties burdened with bank loans would need to be shed to facilitate his transition. With a shrewd eye for business, he strategically divested himself of these properties, ensuring a clean slate for his impending journey.

Yet amidst the flurry of transactions, Dr. Prakash remained mindful of the valuable assets he had cultivated over the years. Properties free from the shackles of debt, steadfastly generating income, were retained as pillars of stability amidst the upheaval of change.

In the streets of America, Dr. Prakash had grown accustomed to the relentless rhythm of life—an existence characterized by long hours spent tending to the needs of his patients, often stretching well into the depths of the night. Yet, as the sands of time carried him back to his homeland India, on 15, December, 1988, Dr. Prakash found himself immersed in a new chapter of existence—a chapter defined not by the frenetic pace of work, but by a harmonious balance of duty, devotion, and community engagement.

In the vibrant city of Indore, where the bustling markets hummed with the melody of life, Dr. Prakash embraced a new rhythm—a rhythm dictated not by the tick-tock of the clock, but by the gentle cadence of the heart. With his practice limited to the morning hours, from 9 am to 1 pm, Dr. Prakash found himself blessed with the gift of time—time to savor the simple joys of life, time to reconnect with loved ones, and time to immerse himself in the rich tapestry of social and religious activities that adorned the fabric of Indian society.

Everyday, as the afternoon sun casted its golden glow over the city, Dr. Prakash found himself drawn to the vibrant pulse of community life, eagerly participating in social gatherings, religious ceremonies, and charitable endeavors that enriched his soul and nourished his spirit.

From volunteering at local charities to attending spiritual discourses, Dr. Prakash embraced each opportunity with an open heart and a spirit of boundless generosity, savoring every moment of connection and camaraderie.

In this newfound rhythm of life, Dr. Prakash discovered a sense of fulfillment that transcended the confines of his professional endeavors —a fulfillment rooted in the bonds of community, the richness of tradition, and the timeless wisdom of ancient teachings. And as he walked the streets of Indore, his heart brimming with gratitude and contentment, Dr. Prakash knew that he had found his place in the intricate tapestry of Indian life—a place where the rhythms of work and leisure, duty and devotion, blended seamlessly together to create a symphony of life lived in harmony with the universe.

08

Challenges of Change

As Dr. Prakash settled back into the rhythms of life in Indore, he found himself confronted with a stark reality—a reality shaped by the harsh contours of scarcity and bureaucracy that seemed to pervade every aspect of daily existence. From the mundane task of purchasing a new car to the simple luxury of owning a gas stove, the hurdles seemed insurmountable, the waiting lists interminable.

For a man who had spent over two decades navigating the smooth highways of America, where convenience was king and efficiency reigned supreme, the contrast was jarring—a bitter reminder of the stark disparities that often defined life in the developing world. Yet, amidst the frustrations and disappointments, Dr. Prakash remained resolute, determined to weather the storm and carve out a life of purpose and meaning in his homeland.

With a steely resolve born of resilience and determination, Dr. Prakash made a solemn vow to himself—he would not succumb to the allure of easy escape, nor would he abandon the land of his birth in pursuit of greener pastures. Instead, he chose to confront the challenges head-on, to stand firm in the face of adversity, and to sow the seeds of change in the fertile soil of his community.

Fortune, it seemed, favored the brave, for Dr. Prakash's path intersected with that of an old childhood friend—a man of influence and authority, whose position as the commissioner of the Indore Municipal Corporation afforded him the power to effect change. Upon learning of Dr. Prakash's plight, his friend wasted no time in springing into action, his words ringing with a mix of disbelief and determination. "You are a fool," he exclaimed, his voice a potent blend of frustration and incredulity. And with those words, the wheels of change were set in motion.

In a remarkable display of friendship and solidarity, Dr. Prakash's friend orchestrated a series of interventions, ensuring that the barriers to progress were swiftly dismantled.

From securing a new car to expediting the installation of a telephone and ensuring a steady supply of gas for his home, Dr. Prakash's friend proved to be a guardian angel in the midst of adversity—a beacon of hope amidst the darkness of despair. And as Dr. Prakash gazed upon the fruits of their collective efforts, he felt a surge of gratitude and renewed determination coursing through his veins—a reminder that in the face of adversity, true friendship and unwavering resolve could conquer even the most formidable of challenges.

Revolutionizing Orthopedics in Indore

In the busy corridors of his American office, Dr. Prakash's schedule was a proof of his expertise and renown—a steady stream of patients clamoring for his attention, with waiting lists stretching weeks into the future. Yet, as he traded the familiar comforts of his American practice for the unfamiliar landscape of Indore, Dr. Prakash found himself confronted with a stark reality—a reality characterized not by the hustle and bustle of a thriving practice, but by a silence that echoed through the empty halls of his office.

With hours stretching languidly before him, Dr. Prakash found himself grappling with a sense of disquiet—a nagging feeling that something was missing, that the vibrant pulse of his profession had somehow been muted amidst the quietude of his new surroundings. Despite his best efforts, the trickle of patients remained less, leaving Dr. Prakash with ample time to decide his next move.

Yet amidst the stillness, a flicker of inspiration ignited within Dr. Prakash's heart—a spark of ingenuity born of necessity and fueled by his unwavering determination to effect change. Drawing upon his wealth of experience and expertise garnered over 16 years of practice in the USA, Dr. Prakash recognized an untapped opportunity—a niche waiting to be filled in the landscape of orthopedic surgery in Indore.

With a boldness born of conviction, Dr. Prakash summoned media to his humble abode for a momentous announcement—a press conference that would alter the course of his practice and his life forever. Armed with a display of intricate surgical techniques and cutting-edge equipment, Dr. Prakash showcased his prowess to a captivated audience, weaving a narrative of innovation and excellence that captured the imagination of all who bore witness.

As the headlines blazed across the front pages of the local newspaper, heralding the dawn of a new era in orthopedic surgery in Indore, Dr. Prakash's practice experienced a meteoric rise—a surge in demand that surpassed even his wildest expectations. From that pivotal moment onwards, the halls of his office echoed with the bustling energy of patients seeking his expertise, and Dr. Prakash never looked back. In the face of adversity, he had forged a path to success—a testament to the indomitable spirit of determination and resilience that burned brightly within his soul.

An Outstanding Doctor

10

Transforming Practices

As Dr. Bangani delved deeper into the complexities of orthopedic surgery in Madhya Pradesh, he quickly realized that he was treading on uncharted territory—a realm where innovation and tradition collided, and where the echoes of the past traveled the corridors of medical practice. Armed with a wealth of knowledge and expertise honed in the crucible of American residency and practice, Dr. Bangani set out to challenge the status quo and rewrite the script of orthopedic care in his homeland.

With a keen eye for opportunity and a heart brimming with compassion, Dr. Bangani recognized a glaring gap in the prevailing treatment protocols for fractured hips—a gap that left patients languishing in prolonged agony and immobilization. Drawing upon his mastery of advanced techniques and cutting-edge procedures, Dr. Bangani dared to defy convention, proposing a revolutionary approach that promised swifter recovery and enhanced mobility for his patients.

The results were nothing short of miraculous. The first patient, buoyed by Dr. Bangani's innovative approach was walking within a mere two days of surgery, while the second patient regained mobility within two weeks. While the third patient took three months to start walking after his surgery.

Dr. Bangani's explanation challenged the long-standing belief that immobilizing patients after a fracture fix was the best course of action. Instead, he advocated for early mobilization, highlighting the benefits of movement in promoting faster recovery and better outcomes. By presenting compelling evidence and demonstrating successful cases, he convinced his colleagues to embrace this innovative approach, ultimately revolutionizing the standard of care in orthopedic surgery.

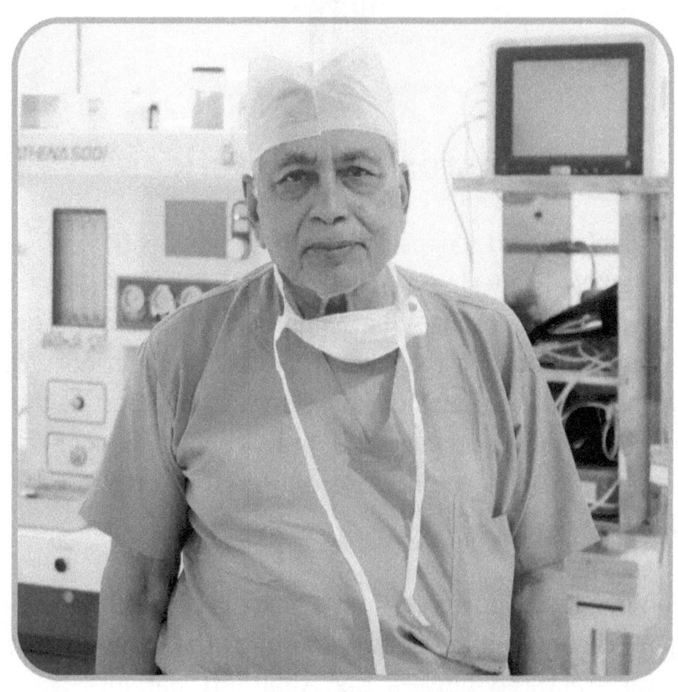

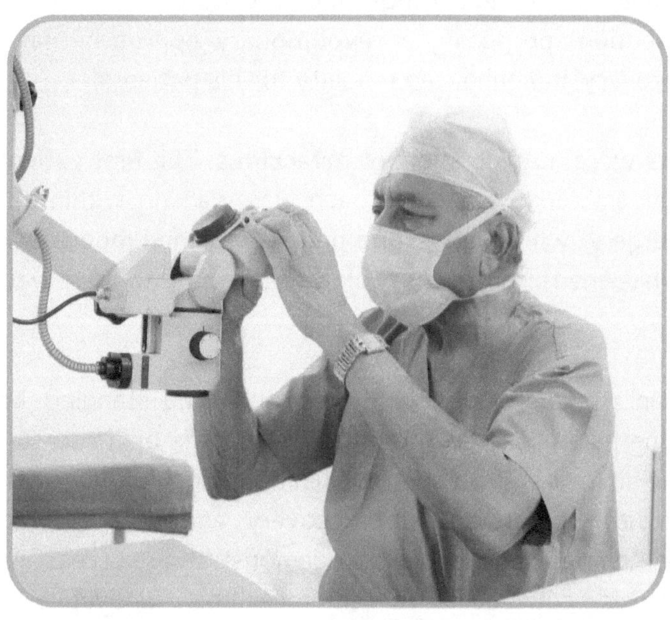

Dr. Bangani's expertise and contributions to the field of orthopedics did not go unnoticed. He was swiftly welcomed as a member of the prestigious Indore Orthopedic Club, where he shared his insights and collaborated with fellow professionals to advance the practice of orthopedic medicine in the region.

Furthermore, Dr. Bangani's dedication to research and scholarly work bore fruit as he authored numerous papers that garnered recognition both nationally and internationally. His publications not only enriched the body of knowledge in orthopedics but also solidified his reputation as a respected authority in the field.

And so, Dr. Bangani's legacy was born—a legacy of compassion, innovation, and hope that would echo through the halls of medicine for years to come. For in the story of Dr. Bangani, we find not just the tale of a remarkable physician, but the timeless reminder that within each of us lies the power to change the world, one courageous act at a time.

Legacy of Excellence

Dr. Prakash Bangani's journey from the bustling medical corridors of America back to the vibrant landscape of India was not merely a geographical transition but a testament to his commitment to excellence in patient care. With 25 years of training and practice in the United States, Dr. Bangani brought back with him a wealth of experience, knowledge, and a profound dedication to upholding the highest standards of ethics and professionalism in the field of medicine.

From the moment he set foot on Indian soil, Dr. Bangani's sincerity, discipline, and accountability towards his profession became evident. His approach to patient management was marked by a rare blend of compassion and clinical expertise, earning him the admiration and respect of both patients and peers alike. Every interaction with Dr. Bangani was imbued with a sense of trust, faith, and commitment to the well-being of his patients.

What truly set Dr. Bangani apart was not just his medical prowess, but his innate ability to connect with people on a deeply human level. His rapport with patients was built on a foundation of empathy, understanding, and genuine concern for their welfare. Whether it was holding a patient's hand during a difficult diagnosis or taking the time to listen attentively to their concerns, Dr. Bangani epitomized the essence of compassionate care.

But Dr. Bangani's dedication extended far beyond the confines of the patient-doctor relationship. He was also a pillar of support and mentorship for his colleagues, treating them with the same respect and honor that he afforded his patients. Despite his years of experience and expertise, Dr. Bangani remained remarkably humble, always willing to lend a listening ear and offer guidance to junior colleagues.

His humility was not just a facade but a genuine reflection of his character, evident in the countless instances where he went above and beyond to uplift and inspire those around him. Whether it was sharing his knowledge and expertise in medical conferences or taking the time to mentor young doctors, Dr. Bangani's generosity knew no bounds.

In the fast-paced world of modern medicine, where compassion often takes a back seat to efficiency, Dr. Bangani stood out as a beacon of hope and humanity. His commitment to ethical patient care and unwavering professionalism served as a guiding light for the medical community, inspiring all those who had the privilege of crossing his path.

As Dr. Bangani continues to practice medicine in India, his legacy of excellence and compassion will undoubtedly endure, leaving an indelible mark on the hearts and minds of all those he has touched.

Savior
of
Vipin Jain

12

A Ray of Hope Amidst Darkness

In the realm of medicine, doctors are revered as modern-day miracle workers, possessing an extraordinary ability to not only combat diseases but also to instill hope and vitality in those grappling with health challenges. These healthcare heroes stand as beacons of light amidst the darkness of illness, offering not just treatment but a lifeline of hope to patients and their families.

However, within medical care, there exist rare and remarkable moments where these healers transcend their role as mere practitioners, becoming emblematic figures of inspiration and resilience. These are the instances that resonate deeply, where doctors become the catalysts for transformation, igniting within their patients the belief in the possibility of a brighter future, the realization of long-held dreams, and the unwavering determination to overcome adversity.

It is in these moments of profound connection and compassion that the true essence of medicine is revealed. Such is the case of Vipin Jain and Dr. Prakash Bangani. Beyond the sterile confines of clinics and operating rooms, Dr. Bangani became the conduits of hope for Vipin, guiding him through the darkest of times and illuminating the path towards healing and recovery.

CA Vipin Jain's life underwent a profound transformation under the unwavering care of Dr. Prakash Bangani. Born to a poor, but very caring parents on 18th December 1975 in the quaint village of Limdi in Gujarat's Dahod District, Vipin Jain's journey commenced amidst a formidable challenge—pulverized by poliomyelitis at the tender age of 8 months, both his lower limbs were left incapacitated. Imprisoned by immobility, he spent his formative years either crawling on the floor like an animal or navigating the terrain on a tricycle, his knees contorted at severe angles, hindering any semblance of mobility.

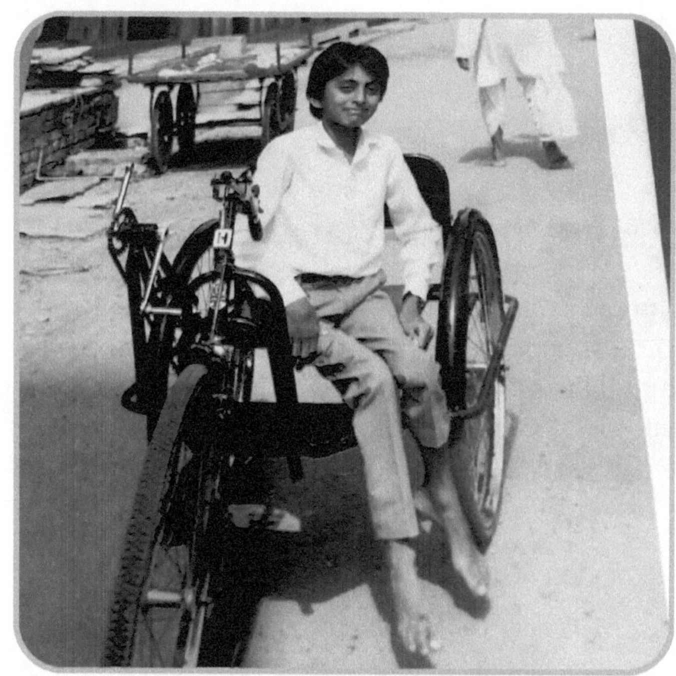

Early Life of Vipin Jain

Saviour and Warrior celebrating 25
years together

The turning point in Vipin's life arrived on 8th July 1994, when he crossed paths with Dr. Prakash Bangani at his Medicare clinic in Indore. Despite the protracted wait and the clinic's closing hours drawing near, the esteemed doctor, to the astonishment of onlookers, imparted a profound assurance to Vipin with a single, resounding phrase, "Me Tujhe Chala Dunga" (I will make you walk), without even laying eyes on his legs. These transformative words kindled a flicker of hope within Vipin, propelling him onto a trajectory of metamorphosis—from crawling on the floor to soaring through the skies, skydiving from a staggering altitude of 14,000 feet.

Under Dr. Bangani's meticulous care, Vipin underwent a series of intricate surgical procedures, encompassing knee contracture releases, hip and knee reconstructions, Triple Arthrodesis and transfer of Peyronie, HTO (Suggested by Dr. K.T. Dholakia), Reconstruction of knee joint, Osteotomy of Tibia with Dr. Sancheti, Osteotomy of Tibia & Femur with Dr. Dror Paley (World Authority in deformity correction), and Osteotomy of Tibia by Dr. Dror Paley (USA). Remarkably, amidst the rigors of medical intervention, Vipin persevered with his studies and triumphantly attained the distinction of a Chartered Accountant in 2002. Today, he stands as a beacon of resilience and determination, an independent globetrotter and accomplished entrepreneur, spearheading his own enterprise with a dedicated team of 50 individuals across diverse locations.

Vipin's odyssey from the depths of adversity to the pinnacle of triumph serves as a poignant testament to the profound impact of a doctor's altruistic care on a patient's life. Dr. Bangani's commitment to Vipin's well-being epitomizes the quintessence of medical professionalism and compassion, underscoring how a doctor transcends the conventional role of a healer to emerge as a veritable guardian angel in the life of a patient.

An Ideal Teacher

13

Orthopedic Pedagogy

The return of Dr. Prakash Bangani to his homeland, Indore, marked the beginning of a transformative era in orthopedic surgery. Before his arrival, the field in Indore was dominated by traditional and conservative treatments, characterized by immobilization of fractures with plasters, prolonged bed rest, and a high level of patient suffering. The orthopedic landscape was shaped by legends such as Dr. Murthy, Dr. R.C. Verma, Dr. Inamdar, Dr. Ohri, and Dr. D.K. Taneja, who achieved remarkable success using conventional methods. However, Dr. Bangani's introduction of innovative techniques brought about revolutionary changes that redefined the field.

One of Dr. Bangani's most significant contributions was the introduction of closed surgical fixation of fractures using image intensifiers, a minimally invasive technique that drastically reduced complications associated with prolonged bed rest. This approach led to limited incisions, minimal tissue trauma, reduced blood loss, and fewer infections. The traditional need for plaster immobilization was eliminated, minimizing risks such as bed sores, pneumonia, deep vein thrombosis (DVT), and pulmonary embolism. Despite the challenges in procuring the necessary instruments and implants—mostly sourced from the USA—Dr. Bangani's determination ensured that these advanced techniques were made available to his patients.

Surgical success is often the result of strong teamwork, and Dr. Bangani found an ideal partner in Dr. Praveen Agrawal, who joined him in 1991 and remained his dedicated disciple. Their partnership extended beyond the operating room, influencing the broader society through their shared commitment to improving patient care. Dr. Bangani introduced the radical idea that surgery should only be performed if the patient could be mobilized and walk postoperatively—a concept that changed the landscape of orthopedic surgery in the region.

An Empathetic listener and relentless motivator..

Dr. Bangani also pioneered the development of subspecialties and super-specialties within orthopedic surgery. He was instrumental in establishing fields such as hand surgery, arthroscopic surgery of joints, joint replacement, and trauma surgery. His leadership inspired a new generation of orthopedic surgeons to seek fellowship positions under his guidance, with many young postgraduates aspiring to learn from his expertise.

Under Dr. Bangani's influence, Indore emerged as a significant center for orthopedic surgery in India. Conferences, workshops, and training modules became integral to the education of new surgeons, heralding an era marked by continuous learning, research, and innovation. The evolution of orthopedic surgery in Madhya Pradesh can indeed be attributed to the "Dr. Prakash Bangani era."

Recognizing the lack of a dedicated orthopedic institution in Madhya Pradesh, Dr. Bangani envisioned the creation of a world-class hospital specializing solely in orthopedic surgery. This vision led to the establishment of Arihant Hospital, despite the political and administrative challenges he faced. With the support of Dr. Praveen Agrawal and Mr. Vishnu Gupta, who brought invaluable expertise in hospital management, the trio worked tirelessly to bring this dream to fruition.

Arihant Hospital quickly became a pilgrimage site for orthopedic trainees and patients, standing as a testament to their service to society. To further advance the field, Dr. Bangani introduced the Diplomate of National Board (DNB) courses at Arihant Hospital. Along with Dr. D.K. Taneja, he developed a crash course for aspiring surgeons, which became one of the most sought-after training programs in India. Dr. Bangani also served as a national examiner for DNB exams, traveling across the country to conduct them. He believed deeply in the responsibility to transfer knowledge to the next generation—a philosophy that was revolutionary at the time.

Dr. Bangani's role as a teacher and mentor was as impactful as his contributions to surgery.

His approach to education was akin to that of a nurturing parent, guiding his students with patience and care. Under his tutelage, students were exposed to groundbreaking innovations and surgical techniques, expanding their skills and broadening their horizons. His teachings went beyond technical expertise, instilling in his students a profound sense of compassion and humanity.

Many of Dr. Bangani's students have gone on to achieve great success, including Shailesh Gupta, who has become the foremost hand surgeon in Madhya Pradesh. Dr. Praveen Agrawal and Dr. Sudhir Chhajed also benefited immensely from Dr. Bangani's mentorship, gaining invaluable insights and expertise that laid the foundation for their successful careers in orthopedics. Rajesh Sharma, one of Dr. Bangani's earliest disciples, exemplifies the transformative power of mentorship. Despite financial constraints, Rajesh was determined to learn from Dr. Bangani, a decision that led him to carve a successful path in England.

Dr. Bangani's legacy extends far beyond the confines of the operating room. His teachings continue to resonate with his students, shaping their professional lives and personal character. He instilled in them a sense of responsibility, empathy, and a commitment to excellence—values that they carry forward in their own practices.

Dr. Prakash Bangani's influence on the field of orthopedic surgery, his dedication to patient care, and his commitment to nurturing the next generation of medical professionals have left an indelible mark on the world. His legacy will continue to inspire and guide future generations, serving as a testament to the extraordinary life of a true master, mentor, and humanitarian.

The Bedrock of Strength and Support

14

Mother: The Guiding Force

Since childhood, Dr. Bangani had imbibed the value of generosity, instilled in him by his parents, particularly his mother, whose guiding light illuminated his path through life's journey. Upon his return to India, Dr. Bangani initially intended to continue his medical practice and relish quality time with family and friends. However, a pivotal conversation with his mother altered his perspective.

One day, his mother posed a seemingly abrupt question about his future plans. Initially taken aback, Dr. Bangani gathered his thoughts and shared his intention to persist with his medical practice. To his surprise, his mother's response was not what he had expected. She inquired about his financial security and, upon hearing his reassurance, gently conveyed her belief that he was already well-established.

In a profound moment, his mother revealed her three heartfelt wishes for him to fulfill. Firstly, she expressed her desire for him to build a hospital to cater to the needs of the less fortunate, ensuring they receive proper medical care. Secondly, she envisioned the establishment of an educational institute, fostering knowledge and empowerment within the community. Lastly, she longed for the creation of a Dharmshala, providing sanctuary for saints and seekers on their spiritual journey.

Moved by his mother's selfless aspirations, Dr. Bangani embarked on a new mission—one driven not only by professional success but also by a deeper sense of purpose and compassion for those in need. With his mother's wishes as his guiding beacon, he set out to make a meaningful difference in the lives of others, honoring the values instilled in him since childhood.

Despite the accolades and recognition he receives for his contributions to society, Dr. Bangani remains steadfast in attributing his motivation and inspiration to his parents. Their humility and simplicity have served as the guiding principles behind his noble endeavors, shaping his character and instilling within him a deep sense of compassion and empathy for others.

In true humility, Dr. Bangani deflects any credit for his own noble works, instead choosing to crown others for his achievements. He acknowledges that his successes are not solely his own but are the result of the collective efforts and support of those around him. It is this self-effacing attitude that endears him to all who have the privilege of knowing him, as he embodies the true essence of humility and gratitude in every aspect of his life and work.

15

Family as a Pillar

Dr. Bangani's journey towards becoming a respected doctor and compassionate philanthropist was a collaborative effort, fueled by the unwavering support of his family, particularly his devoted wife and three daughters.

On December 11, 1963, Prakash married Saroj, a woman of remarkable intelligence and resilience hailing from Sadri, Rajasthan. Though her formal education was limited to high school, Saroj possessed a sharp intellect and boundless determination.

Together, they ventured across the seas to America, where Prakash pursued his medical residency. Yet, their early days in a foreign land were fraught with financial challenges, with Prakash's meager salary of $135 per month barely sufficient to cover their expenses. Recognizing the need to augment their income, Saroj took matters into her own hands. She enrolled in English classes and secured employment in a factory, where she toiled tirelessly for four years. Undeterred by the demands of her job, Saroj later transitioned to selling cosmetics, exhibiting grit and determination as she traversed door to door to peddle her wares. Through her unwavering dedication, Saroj not only contributed significantly to the family finances but also emerged as a beacon of strength and resilience in the face of adversity.

With her steadfast support, their humble abode blossomed into a sanctuary of joy and tranquility, where love and laughter filled every corner. As their family grew to include three daughters - Sangita, Anita, and Asha - the Bangani household brimmed with warmth and familial bliss.

Dr. Prakash with his wife Saroj
Together in all seasons, every moment is a
cherished memory

Throughout their 58 years of marriage, Saroj remained Prakash's steadfast companion and confidante, sharing in every triumph and tribulation that life presented. Together, they weathered storms, celebrated victories, and forged an unbreakable bond anchored in love, trust, and mutual respect. Saroj's steadfast presence, unwavering faith, and constant support were the cornerstones of their enduring partnership, embodying the true essence of companionship and unity.

In addition to his wife's unwavering support, Dr. Bangani was fortunate to have the backing of his family. Their encouragement and guidance played a crucial role in his journey towards realizing his aspirations in Indore. Whether it was offering practical assistance in managing the clinic or providing emotional support during times of uncertainty, his family's unwavering presence bolstered his confidence and fueled his ambition.

With the love and support of his family as his foundation, Dr. Bangani's vision for his practice in Indore began to take shape. Their collective efforts and unwavering belief in his abilities served as a driving force, propelling him towards his goals and solidifying his place within the community as a trusted and respected healthcare provider.

Visionary Foundations

16

Arihant Hospital & Research Centre

Dr. Prakash Bangani embarked on a remarkable journey guided by his mother's wisdom, driven by a vision to establish a healthcare facility that would transcend borders and bring world-class medical expertise to the doorstep of those in need. With unwavering determination and a heart full of compassion, he laid the foundation of Arihant Hospital and Research Centre in 2002, spanning across 2 acres of land.

At its inception, Arihant Hospital housed 110 beds, but under Dr. Bangani's visionary leadership, it has evolved into a robust healthcare facility boasting 155 beds and more than 12 OPD chambers, complemented by a dedicated team of over 200 supporting staff. Rooted in the profound Sanskrit mantra "Sarvetra Sukhina: Santu, Sarve Santu Niramaya", which translates to "Let all be blissful, Let all stay healthy," the hospital's mission resonates deeply with its motto: "More than Healthcare, Human Care."

Driven by a relentless pursuit of excellence, Arihant Hospital has positioned itself as a beacon of hope and healing in Madhya Pradesh, offering a comprehensive range of services spanning orthopedics, hand surgery, renal dialysis, and more. Renowned for its expertise in joint replacement surgeries, the hospital's Joint Replacement Centre in Indore stands as a testament to its commitment to delivering quality care at an affordable price.

The hospital's state-of-the-art operation theaters, built to international standards, are equipped with cutting-edge technology, including laminar flow systems and individual air handling units, ensuring a sterile environment conducive to complex surgical procedures. With a focus on transparency and affordability, Arihant Hospital offers fixed packages for knee transplants, providing patients with peace of mind and eliminating the burden of hidden charges.

Arihant Hospital and Research Centre

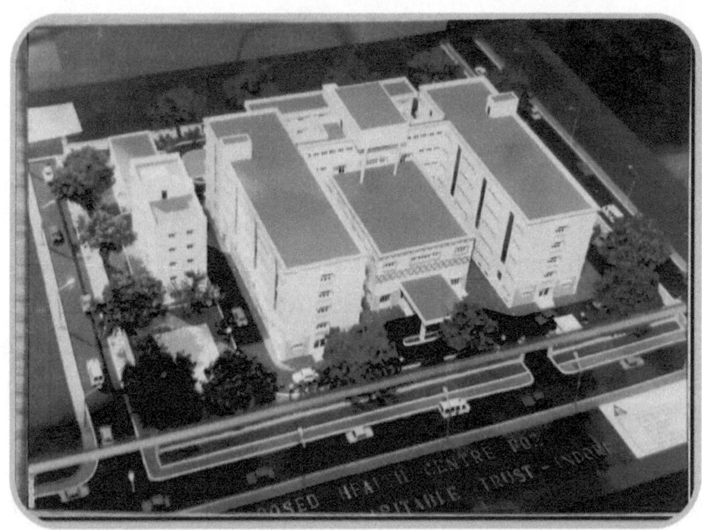

Dreams turn into reality one step at a time

When dreams become accomplishments

Dr. Prakash with Minister Digvijaya Singh

Dr. Prakash with Minister Kailash Vijaywargiya

Beyond its clinical services, Arihant Hospital serves as a hub for education and community outreach, offering courses in OT technology, postgraduate training in orthopedics, and specialized training programs for law enforcement and corporate professionals. Dr. Bangani's commitment to nurturing the next generation of healthcare professionals underscores his dedication to advancing medical education and promoting road safety awareness in the community.

Arihant Hospital, under its Sanjeevani Sena Scheme, provides charity to help vulnerable people who cannot afford proper treatment. The hospital has performed around 127 free knee replacements, the highest number in the city.

The Department of Orthopedics, a cornerstone of Arihant Hospital and Research Center, has been a trailblazer in medical training, boasting accreditation for Diplomate of National Board (DNB) programs from 2006 to 2019, with an impressive track record of 27 successful candidates. Additionally, the department has produced two DNB Family Medicine graduates, further cementing its reputation for academic excellence. In response to the evolving healthcare landscape, the Department of Medicine has recently been accredited for NBEMS DNB programs, with plans underway to expand offerings in Anesthesia and Family Medicine.

Complementing its academic prowess, Arihant Hospital and Research Center also houses the Samarpan College of Nursing, offering comprehensive BSc and MSc courses since 2015. Recognizing the importance of practical experience, the college organizes regular Continuing Medical Education (CME) sessions, workshops, and on-the-job training programs for doctors, nurses, and allied healthcare professionals. Encouraging active participation in conferences and workshops, students are provided with opportunities to broaden their horizons and gain invaluable real-world experience through observer roles at higher centers.

Arihant Hospital and Research Centre

Library: Arihant Hospital and Research Centre

Overseeing the academic affairs of the college is a dedicated committee led by esteemed professionals such as Prof. DK Taneja, a former Dean of MGM Medical College Indore and renowned orthopedic surgeon, along with Prof. Prakash Bangani, a senior orthopedic surgeon serving as the Managing Director. Together with departmental faculties, meeting coordinators, and senior doctors, this committee ensures the seamless functioning of academic activities while upholding the highest standards of ethics and student welfare.

With departments spanning Medicine, Pediatrics, and Obstetrics and Gynecology, Arihant Hospital and Research Center remains committed to nurturing the next generation of healthcare professionals, guided by a steadfast commitment to excellence and innovation in medical education. As it continues to expand its academic offerings and uphold its tradition of academic excellence, it remains at the forefront of shaping the future of healthcare education in India.

As of now, Arihant Hospital and Research Centre has become one of the most economic and best Orthopedic and Hand surgery in Madhya Pradesh.

17

Shri Jain Shwetambar Academy

Dr. Prakash Bangani owned a piece of land, and one of his close friends suggested that he utilize it to establish an educational institution. This led to the foundation of Shri Jain Shwetambar Academy. Dr. Bangani has been a vital part of the school's board, regularly attending board meetings and participating in important events like Independence Day.

The college is spread across 6.5 acres, with a constructed area of 48,910 square feet and a vast 210,000 square-foot playground. It boasts 39 rooms, including 8 fully equipped laboratories and two magnificent auditoriums, each covering 4,500 square feet. In addition, the campus has ample parking, lush green gardens, and sufficient space for both indoor and outdoor sports. The location is ideal for educational purposes, offering a pollution-free, peaceful, and natural environment.

Since its establishment in 2006, the college has successfully offered several undergraduate degree and diploma courses. The vision of Shri Jain Shwetambar Academy is to be a premier, quality education-oriented learning center. The institution maintains high standards and expectations for its students.

The college is affiliated with Devi Ahilya Vishwavidyalaya, Indore (M.P.) and the Board of Secondary Education, Bhopal (M.P.). It is approved and recognized by the Department of Higher Education, Bhopal (M.P.), and the National Council for Teacher Education, New Delhi.

Living proof that dreams come true

**From dreaming to achieving: a journey of
determination and persistence**

Wel Co
SHRI JA   HWET
PROFESS   AL AC
Aerodram   ss r
15/03/2014

Wel Com
SHRI JAIN SHWETAMB
PROFE   ONAL ACADE
Aerodra   mpur by pass road, Ind
15/03/2014

Beyond Medicine: Social and Religious Involvement

18

Temple of Service

In 1990, Dr. Prakash's elder brother, Shikhar Chand Nagori, recognizing his leadership potential and commitment to community service, nominated him as the representative for the Malwa area in the prestigious national religious organization, Aanandji Kalyanji Pedhi. Winning the election with overwhelming support from the community, Dr. Prakash assumed the mantle of responsibility with a deep sense of duty and dedication.

As the representative, Dr. Prakash embarked on a journey to organize and spearhead various social activities aimed at uplifting and uniting the Jain community. With the generosity of community members contributing through donations, he set out to address pressing issues and promote harmony within the community.

During his tenure, a significant challenge emerged when tensions flared between the Shwetambar and Digambar sects over the sacred Shikharji mountain. Stepping into the fray as a mediator and advocate for unity, Dr. Prakash took on the formidable task of raising awareness and mobilizing support within the community to safeguard their religious heritage.

Driven by his vision of fostering unity amidst diversity, Dr. Prakash brought together leaders from all six Jain units, transcending differences to form the Akhil Bharatiya Shwetambar Jain Mahasangh, the idea was to unite the entire Shwetambar community. This bold initiative served as a rallying point for the community, empowering them to stand united against external threats and preserve their shared cultural and religious identity.

The essence of well-being lies in nurturing the spirit

To further strengthen bonds and promote cultural solidarity, Dr. Prakash conceptualized and orchestrated a series of impactful initiatives. Among these was the grand procession of Mahavir Jayanti, a vibrant and celebratory event that drew thousands of participants, igniting a sense of pride and belonging within the community.

Additionally, Dr. Prakash organized the harmonious gathering of saints and community leaders during the auspicious occasion of Paryushan, creating a platform for dialogue, reflection, and spiritual enrichment. His adept leadership and diplomatic skills played a pivotal role in fostering cooperation and understanding among diverse factions within the community.

Introducing innovative programs like the Samuhik Tiffin Party, a communal lunch held at Nehru Park, Dr. Prakash sought to cultivate a sense of camaraderie and inclusivity, bringing people together in a spirit of fellowship and goodwill. The overwhelming success of these initiatives underscored his ability to inspire and mobilize collective action for the greater good.

Dr. Prakash's commitment to serving the Jain community extended beyond his role as a representative. From 1992 to 2013, he assumed the presidency of the Shwetambar Samaj, a position that entrusted him with the responsibility of overseeing and supporting various community initiatives and projects.

Under his leadership, the Shwetambar Samaj played a crucial role in maintaining and preserving Jain temples across India. Dr. Prakash's tireless efforts and unwavering dedication to the cause exemplified the highest ideals of service and devotion, earning him the respect and admiration of his peers and community members alike.
Prakash is also a trustee of a fund that runs several mandirs. The fund has over $1 billion that Prakash helps manage.

19

Impact Beyond Medicine

Driven by a profound sense of duty and compassion, Dr. Prakash took on the role of secretary within the Mahasangh, leading a dedicated team in a multitude of philanthropic endeavors aimed at uplifting their Jain community. Their journey began with a focus on education, assuming responsibility for the academic welfare of underprivileged children. With meticulous care, they covered the academic fees of these children, ensuring they had the opportunity to pursue their studies unhindered. This noble initiative, initiated by Dr. Prakash and his team, continues unabated, with detailed records maintained for each student, including their personal information and contact details, a testament to their enduring commitment to the cause.

Expanding their scope of assistance, Dr. Prakash and his team extended health coverage to those without access to insurance, providing vital support in times of medical need. Additionally, on the auspicious occasion of Mahavir Jayanti, they orchestrate grand gatherings where nutritious meals are distributed to thousands in attendance, a heartwarming display of communal solidarity and generosity. What began as a modest gathering for 4000 individuals has blossomed into a monumental event, now serving upwards of 22,000 to 24,000 individuals annually.

Recognizing the critical need for blood donations, the Mahasangh has been organizing blood donation camps every year, a lifeline for those in urgent need of transfusions. Over the years, the budget for these noble endeavors has grown exponentially, from a modest 50,000 to an impressive 50 lakh, all sourced from generous donations from the community. In the early years, Dr. Prakash himself traveled to different neighborhoods, personally soliciting donations and issuing receipts for contributions as small as 100 rupees.

As their team expanded and contributions surged, they established a membership program in 2002, inviting financially stable individuals to join the cause by contributing 5000 rupees each.

Empowered by the support of their community, Dr. Prakash and his team reached a significant milestone in 2005, eliminating the need for external fundraising efforts as their social projects became entirely self-sustaining. Buoyed by this success, they secured a dedicated office space in 2007, further solidifying their presence and impact within the community. Guided by the wisdom of his mother, Dr. Prakash also embarked on the construction of Upashrays and Dharamshalas, providing sanctuaries where saints from across the country could find solace and respite, a testament to his enduring commitment to service and compassion.

20

Bhagwan Mahavir Viklang Sahayata Samiti

For more than a decade now, Dr. Prakash has been an integral part of the Bhagwan Mahavir Viklang Sahayata Samiti,the Jaipur foot which has been rendering invaluable service to the community, touching the lives of over 10,000 patients with its unwavering commitment to provide absolute free assistance. Beyond merely providing medical aid, the organization goes the extra mile by offering free lodging and boarding to patients from outside Indore, ensuring that they receive comprehensive care and support during their stay.

At the heart of the Samiti's operations lies the noble endeavor of crafting artificial limbs, a process that begins with meticulous measurements and culminates in the creation of custom-made limbs and calipers tailored to each patient's unique needs. This meticulous approach to prosthetic manufacturing ensures optimal functionality and comfort for every individual.

The organization's efforts have not gone unnoticed, with dignitaries such as the Minister for Women and Child Development taking a keen interest in its activities. Witnessing firsthand the process of limb fitment and observing the transformative impact it has on patients, these leaders have lauded the Samiti's dedication to improving the lives of the differently-abled.

As the Mahavir Viklang Sahayata Samiti continues its noble mission, it remains steadfast in its commitment to serving humanity with compassion and dignity, ensuring that every individual, regardless of their circumstances, receives the care and support they need to live life to the fullest.

In addition to its remarkable efforts in prosthetic manufacturing, the Bhagwan Mahavir Viklang Sahayata Samiti extends its compassionate care to children with dislocated joints, offering them specialized treatment to alleviate their discomfort and restore mobility. This comprehensive approach to healthcare ensures that individuals with a diverse range of orthopedic challenges receive the attention and support they need to lead fulfilling lives.

Furthermore, the Samiti's impact transcends borders, with approximately 200 surgeries performed free of cost. Through these surgeries, countless individuals have been given a new lease on life, empowered to pursue their dreams and aspirations with renewed confidence.

The scope of the Mahavir Viklang Sahayata Samiti's impact is truly staggering, with an estimated 14,000 patients receiving treatment within its walls. This staggering number underscores the organization's unwavering commitment to serving humanity, offering hope and healing to those in need irrespective of their background or circumstances. As a beacon of compassion and solidarity, the Samiti continues to embody the spirit of service, touching hearts and transforming lives with its selfless dedication to the well-being of all.

Artificial limbs making in process

Fitment of limbs

A girl child walked for the First time
with artificial limb

Achievements

21

Achievements, Leadership, and Lasting Impact

Educational Qualifications

- MS in General Surgery (1967)
- Board Certification in Orthopedic Surgery (USA, 1971)
- Fellowship in Hand Surgery (USA, 1972)

Professional Positions

- **In the USA:**
    - Vice President of Orthopedic Association of West Virginia
    - Member of American Society of Hand Surgeons
    - Assistant Professor of Orthopedic Surgery, University of West Virginia
- **In India:**
    - President of Indore Orthopedic Association

Social Contributions

- **In the USA:**
    - Foundation Member of India Centre, Charleston, West Virginia
- **In India:**
    - Founder & President, Shri Shwetambar Jain Mahasangh (MP, 1994-2013)
    - Central Council Member, Anandji Kalyanji Pedi, Ahmedabad (1993-present)
    - President, Arihant Hospital and Research Centre
    - President, Shwetambar Jain Academy
    - Chairman, Arihant Urban Co-operative Bank

BHOPA
42ND | ANNUAL CONFERENCE
CHAPTER IOA
MPIOA
BHOPA

Religious Leadership

- Managing Director, Jain Shantinath Mandir, Bhopawar
- Managing Director, Maksi Jain Teerth (1996-2002)
- Managing Director, Ujjain, Kharakua Shwetambar Jain Mandir Trust (2006-2013)
- President, Shri Shwetambar Jain Tapgrah Upashray (2017-present)

Key Contributions to Rehabilitation and Orthopedics

- Rehabilitation Pioneer: Revolutionized early preventive measures for faster recovery in patients.
- Orthoses & Prosthetics Innovator: Introduced modern treatments for orthoses and prosthetics, significantly improving the quality of life for physically challenged individuals.

Awards and Recognitions

- **Chikitsa Seva Award (2004):** For outstanding service in healthcare.
- **Devi Ahilya Award:** Presented by Shri Adwani ji for his broader societal contributions.
- **Humanitarian Award (2024): First-ever recipient** of this prestigious award in the history of the Madhya Pradesh Orthopaedic Surgeons Society (MPIOA), conferred at the 42nd Annual Conference in Bhopal. This award highlights Dr. Prakash Bangani's exceptional contributions to healthcare and his humanitarian efforts.

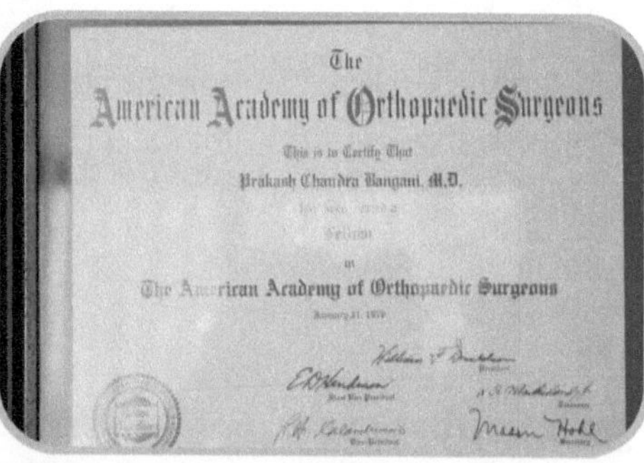

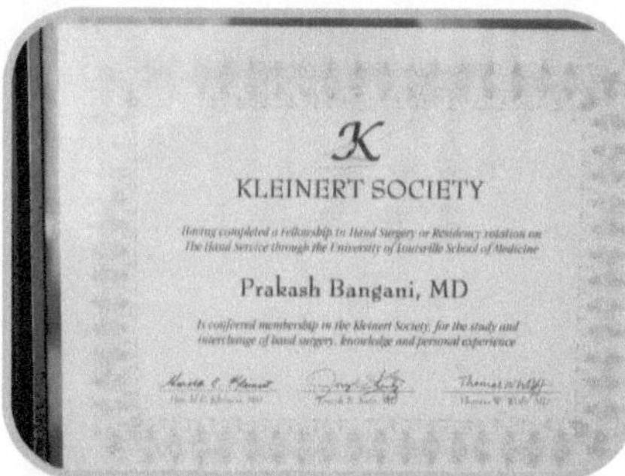

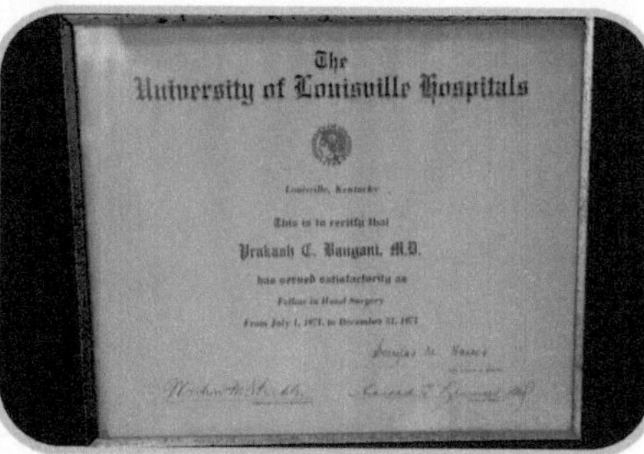

A Timeless Inspiration

22

Monk in the World of Orthopedics

Dr. Prakash's journey through the corridors of medicine is not merely a tale of professional success; it's a symphony of dedication, resilience, and unwavering love for humanity. From the gleaming halls of American hospitals to the humble clinics of his homeland, his story illuminates the transformative power of one individual's commitment to service.

With each step, Dr. Prakash painted his canvas with the colors of compassion and determination. His decision to return to India wasn't about comfort or convenience; it was a calling, a profound sense of duty to give back to the land that nurtured his roots. Despite the stark contrast in lifestyles, he traded luxury for purpose, proving that true fulfillment lies in serving others selflessly.

Deep within his heart, there was a yearning, an unquenchable desire to return to the land of his birth. From the very beginning, he held an unwavering conviction that he would one day return to India and contribute to its growth. Even though India might not have been as advanced as America during those times, it did not diminish his passion and commitment towards his homeland.

When he returned, the canvas of reality was painted with hues far different from his initial plans. Once a man basking in comfort, with his own car and an array of amenities at his disposal, he now found himself wrestling for basic luxuries like gas and telephone. Yet, he willingly traded his cushioned existence to embrace the call of his homeland. He chose to dedicate the rest of his life serving its people - a testament to the power of love for one's nation over personal comfort.

In the midst of challenges, Dr. Prakash didn't falter. Instead, he embraced them as opportunities to make a difference.

His orthopedic expertise became a beacon of hope for countless souls, transforming lives and reshaping destinies. But beyond his medical prowess, it was his unwavering faith in humanity that set him apart. He didn't just heal bodies; he ignited spirits and inspired change.

As the sun sets on Dr. Prakash's remarkable journey, his legacy shines brighter than ever. He wasn't just a healer; he was a revolutionary force, a living testament to the perfect harmony between science and faith. Through his life, he taught us that true greatness isn't measured by personal accolades but by the lives we touch and the difference we make.

Dr. Prakash Bangani's story isn't just a chapter in the annals of medicine; it's a timeless testament to the power of love, dedication, and service.

Conclusion

Dr. Prakash Bangani, a living embodiment of dedication and selfless service, continues to inspire awe and admiration as he walks the path of healing. His journey, marked by unwavering commitment and boundless compassion, serves as a guiding light for generations to come.

As a family man, Dr. Prakash finds strength and purpose in the love and support of his loved ones. Despite the demands of his profession, he has always prioritized his role as a son, husband, father, friend, and guide nurturing the bonds that sustain him through life's trials and triumphs.

Beyond the confines of his home, Dr. Prakash's impact extends far and wide. As a philanthropist, he channels his resources and expertise towards uplifting the less fortunate, providing hope and healing to those in need. His generosity knows no bounds, his kindness touching the lives of countless individuals across the globe.

But it is as a healer that Dr. Prakash truly shines. With each patient he treats, he embodies the essence of compassion and empathy, offering not just medical care but also solace and support. His dedication to his passion is unwavering, his commitment to excellence unparalleled. In his hands, miracles unfold, lives are transformed, and hope is restored.

Dr. Bangani's journey is a testament to the transformative power of one individual's dedication and selflessness. He is not just a doctor; he is a healer in the truest sense of the word. His life is a testament to the profound impact that one person can have on the world, and his legacy will continue to inspire and uplift for generations to come.

As we celebrate Dr. Prakash Bangani's remarkable achievements and contributions, let us also pause to honor the man behind the accolades – a humble servant of humanity, a beacon of hope, and above all, an extraordinary human being. In a world plagued by division and strife, Dr. Prakash stands as a symbol of unity and humanity.

He reminds us that we are all connected, that our actions have the power to uplift and inspire. His life is a testament to the resilience of the human spirit and the boundless potential for goodness that lies within each of us.

Messages from Loved Ones

"Dad,

You are a constant source of inspiration in every way. Your loving and caring nature has earned you unwavering respect from everyone around you. As a father, you're always there for me when I need you.

Your love for me is evident in the little things you do—like fussing over me when I visit. You take my "getting upset" with you in stride, loving me unconditionally, no matter my tantrums!

You're a generous, loving father and grandfather. Your grandkids adore you and have learned so much from you during their summer vacation visits. I cherish the special bond they share with you.

I'm always inspired by all the charity work you do. We can only hope to follow in your footsteps.

Love you, Dad!"

**Sangita Bafna,
Cleveland, USA**

"Daddy,

I have always held you in the highest respect, love, and admiration. I've learned so much from you since I was a little girl, and I'm inspired not just by your words but by your actions. Your commitment to your work, family, and principles has shaped me into who I am today.

Your achievements in medicine and dedication to serving others through Arihant Hospital have left a permanent mark on my life and our community. I've been fortunate to bring your four older grandsons with me to Indore to spend time with you and Nani. You've developed such a special bond with each of them, making those days in Indore truly special.

To say I'm proud to be Dr. Bangani's daughter is an understatement. Your influence reaches far beyond our family, touching countless lives, and I am honored to carry forward your legacy in my own life."

**Anita Mehta ,
Pittsburgh, USA**

"If there is someone who is both inspirational and aspirational to me, it is my loving father. Courage, determination, charity, kindness, respect, spirituality, and empathy are just a few of the qualities that radiate from him to everyone around him. As a gentle disciplinarian, he commands respect and inspires others to follow his lead. His love for me is unwavering, and he always provides the best advice in times of crisis. He has evolved from being my strict parent to my mentor and guiding compass. Is he everything a father should be? He is as close as one can humanly achieve."

**Asha Pitalia,
Manchester, UK**

"Ever since I became a part of the Bangani family, he has been like a father to me. I lost my own father soon after my marriage. He was more of a friend and father to Mahendra than an uncle and played a significant role in bringing us together. Even today, I always find him by my side, especially when we have lost many members of our family. To all of us, he is the heart of the family—a loving great-grandfather to Aarsh. As a doctor, teacher, and noble human being, he is a source of inspiration for future generations. He is our pride."

Sapna Bangani

"*Kakasa and Babusa never treated any of us eight children differently, and that's exactly what we learned from them. We've always stood united, following their example. Despite being such a renowned doctor, Kakasa always listened to Babusa's words without question or argument.*

These same values and principles were instilled in us. When I moved into a joint family, it was these values and this culture that allowed me to become an integral part of the family.

The respect they showed one another and the way they prioritized family above all else taught me the importance of harmony and togetherness. Their ability to maintain unity within the family has shaped who I am today, allowing me to carry those same principles into my own life and relationships."

Your eldest daughter,

Shobhana Sancheti

"Respected and Dear Kakasa,

Our well-known and prestigious Dr. Prakash Bangani's impressive personality, straightforwardness, fearlessness, sincerity, and hardworking nature, along with his simple living and high thinking, are valuable assets for both our family and society!

I am truly inspired by your constant, dedicated commitment to society on the professional front, and by how you have practically implemented Dharmic teachings in your life! Your positive energy and enthusiasm, even at this age, are qualities I deeply admire and learn from.

We have grown up witnessing Bausa and Kakasa's love, affection, and beautiful bond, which we continue to carry forward in our family. Mummy and Chachi Ji's love will live in our hearts forever.
My visit to Kakasa's place in the US was truly memorable, and I am grateful for the Dharma-related teachings you always share with me and my family.

Your elegant and radiant persona has attracted and impacted many dignitaries in Surat as well!
My family and I love spending quality time with you in Surat, and we cherish the many fun moments we have shared together!
We are truly blessed, grateful, and proud of our Kakasa! Keep inspiring us always!"

Pratibha- Rajesh Jain & Family

"Kakasa,

Words can never fully express what you mean to us. In every area—whether in your profession, the Jain community, or society at large—you have given so much to those in need of support. We feel immense pride in being your children.

As I reflect on this, my thoughts also turn to my dear Chachi ji, without whom this biography would remain incomplete.

Chachi ji and I shared a very special bond. While she loved all the children, our brother was her heartbeat, and I was her most cherished daughter.

I remember you often telling us how, in the early years of your life together—especially when you moved to the U.S. for your medical studies—Chachi ji stood by you with unwavering support. Her presence in our lives was invaluable, and I miss her deeply as I write this.

We are truly blessed to have grown up under the care of the incredible pillars of our family: Babusa, Mummy, you, and Chachi ji."

Your daughter,

Sunita Jain

"Kakasa,

You and Babusaheb have taught us that being a good human being is the most important thing in life. I will always strive to follow in your footsteps and uphold the values you have instilled in me.

You have played an instrumental role in shaping both my personal and professional life. In moments when I felt lost, you understood without me saying a word and gently guided me to find my way.

You have always been an unwavering source of inspiration, not only for our family but for countless others whose lives you have touched.

Your energy, even at this stage of life, is a testament to your remarkable willpower and compassion in helping those in need. I deeply admire and respect this about you.

If we could embody even a fraction of what you have achieved, we would consider our lives truly successful."

Your daughter,

Vinita Puntambekar

"I first met Dr. Prakash Bangani on the 8th of July, 1994, at his Medicare clinic. We had learned about him from a family in our village who had sought his treatment for their daughter. They said, 'Yadi ye Dr. sahab bole ki thik ho jaega to unke bharose chhod do aur bole nahi hoga to duniya me kahi mat jao.' Such was the trust and reverence people had for Dr. Bangani."

On that day, we arrived at his clinic without an appointment. His secretary informed us that Dr. Bangani could not see us without a prior booking. However, we pleaded with her, explaining that we had traveled a long distance. Miraculously, Dr. Bangani agreed to see me even after the clinic had closed for the day.

My brother carried me into the clinic and placed me in a chair before him. The first words Dr. Bangani spoke in his chilly cabin—where I still remember a beautiful picture of him with his family on his desk—were, 'ME TUJHE CHALA DUNGA' And the rest, as they say, is history.

I have been fortunate enough to know Dr. Bangani closely since that day, almost three decades ago. This book captures many facets of his extraordinary life and achievements. But the qualities that I admire most about him are his humbleness, kindness, and selflessness.

One simple example of his humility comes to mind. During our many discussions and meetings in his cabin, I noticed a table in the corner with a water jug and glasses for visitors.

Whenever someone came in, Dr. Bangani would get up from his chair, pour the water, and serve it to the visitor himself. It would have been easy for him to call for assistance, as he had many people available to help. Yet, he chose to serve others personally, reflecting his genuine humility.

I consider myself incredibly fortunate to have had my life transformed by Dr. Bangani. From crawling on the floor like an animal for the first 19 years of my life, he helped me become a respectable human being. He showered me with love and respect, making me a part of his life and family. His unwavering belief in me enabled me to become a board member of his esteemed organizations.

Dr. Prakash Bangani is a beacon of hope and compassion. His life and work are a testament to the profound impact one person can have on the lives of many. This book is a tribute to his remarkable journey and the countless lives he has touched and healed."

CA. Vipin Jain
(Patient since 1994)

"The Malwa region of Indore has nurtured many personalities who have gained global recognition, and one of the most distinguished among them is Dr. Prakash Bangani, a highly respected orthopedic surgeon and dedicated social worker.

Born on April 10, 1941, into a devout Jain family, Dr. Bangani's early life was deeply influenced by the values of religion, social service, and humanity. He grew up in the prominent bullion district of Indore, where these virtues were integral to his upbringing. His elder brother, Shri Shikharchandji Nagauri, served as a guiding light and mentor throughout his life. The bond between the brothers was as strong as the legendary Ram and Lakshman, with their relationship becoming a source of strength for the entire family. Dr. Bangani also shared a deep, affectionate bond with his two sisters, receiving unwavering support and love from them.

In December 1963, Dr. Bangani married Saroj, the daughter of Shri Sheshmalji Rathore from Rajasthan. Shortly after, he completed his MBBS in 1964 and his MS in 1969 from MGM Medical College, Indore. His pursuit of excellence led him to the United States, where he practiced orthopedic surgery until 1971 and later specialized in hand surgery in 1972. His pioneering work in reconstructing a severed thumb using a patient's little finger earned him widespread acclaim. Despite his thriving career in the U.S., Dr. Bangani remained deeply connected to his roots in India, frequently visiting his homeland with his family, which grew to include three daughters—Sangeeta, Anita, and Asha.

After spending 21 successful years in the U.S., Dr. Bangani returned to Indore in 1988 to care for his aging parents.

Upon his return, he resumed his medical practice and devoted himself to teaching, mentoring the next generation of doctors. Alongside his elder brother, he founded the Arihant Charitable Trust, and in 2002, established Arihant Hospital, a 200-bed facility that became renowned for its specialized services. The hospital also became home to the world-renowned Mahavir Handicapped Center, where approximately 12,930 free prosthetic limb transplants have been performed, continuing Dr. Bangani's lasting legacy of philanthropy and service to humanity."

Vishal Dakolia, Indore

"Born into a respectable business family, Dr. Prakash Bangani is married to an intelligent woman and is a proud father of three daughters and grandfather to six grandchildren. He credits his family for instilling values that have guided him throughout his life. His parents often remarked on his maturity beyond his years and his love for books and working with patients.

From a young age, Dr. Bangani knew he wanted to be a doctor. While in college, witnessing numerous accidents and injuries inspired him to pursue medical school. During his clinical rotations, especially in the sports injury clinic, he developed a passion for treating musculoskeletal, bone, connective tissue, and spinal cord issues related to injuries or illness.

Determined to gain the best training possible, he decided to pursue his studies in the United States. There, he underwent extensive training in orthopedic surgery and specialized in hand surgery. He practiced in the U.S. for several years but, aware of his aging parents and driven by a desire to serve his country, he returned to India.

Dr. Bangani came back with a mission to make a positive impact on the lives of those in need of medical care. He envisioned a career where he could use his expertise to bring innovative solutions and meaningful change. With a well-thought-out plan, he decided to build a hospital. He sought donations from friends and family for this charitable cause and, with overwhelming support, successfully established a state-of-the-art hospital.

The hospital provides care not only for orthopedic patients but also addresses a wide range of medical issues, offering significant charitable services to the poor and needy. It employs highly qualified doctors, nurses, and paramedical staff, all committed to providing the best possible care.

Dr. Bangani continues to serve as both an administrator and an orthopedic surgeon, ensuring that every patient receives the attention and care they deserve."

Radhu Agrawal

"Dr. Prakash Bangani – My elder brother,

Dr. Prakash Bangani is a renowned name in his own right. I was first introduced to Dr. Saheb in 1982 when he was working in America. During our first meeting, I attended your lecture on a completely new topic, and I was deeply impressed. Listening to the lecture, I could immediately sense your knowledge and dedication.

In 1988, we heard that after serving in America for 21 years, he had returned to settle in Indore to honor his mother's wishes. To fulfill her dream, he established the state-of-the-art Arihant Hospital in 2002 in the western part of Indore.

Dr. Bangani is credited with pioneering complex surgeries like joint replacement and arthroscopy, as well as training numerous orthopedic specialists in these procedures.

He actively participated in the meetings of the Indore Orthopedic Organization, offering suggestions that were fully respected by the members. After a few years, he took the reins of the organization and led it to new heights.

In 2003, after I retired from the position of Dean, at his request, I began working at Arihant Hospital. Over the past 20 years, I have had the opportunity to get to know Dr. Bangani more closely. He is an exceptionally skilled surgeon, and his compassion, respect, and love for his patients have built deep connections with them. Many of his old patients return to him for consultation even after years.

Together, we transformed Arihant Hospital into a postgraduate institute, launching postgraduate courses for students that received recognition from the Government of India.

Every year, more than 100 orthopedic students are trained here, earning the institute national recognition. Your teaching methods are simple yet highly effective.

We have served as examiners in many examinations together. His straightforward and approachable method of conducting exams has been highly beneficial for the students. He remained sensitive to their needs and made every effort to ensure they succeed. Recognizing his dedication and proactive approach, the National Examination Board appointed him as an inspector for numerous hospitals.

I have personally observed that you gladly accept any good suggestion and always strive to provide affordable and effective treatment to those in need. Despite having your own private hospital, you established the Sanjeevani Sanstha, through which you offer free medical treatment to the poor.

With your support and help, we successfully organized the Indo-German Foundation Meeting and the All India Spine Conference. In 2017, we took on the challenge of hosting a major event, the Annual Conference of the Indian Orthopedic Association, attended by over 5,000 delegates. For two years, you stood by me through every challenge, demonstrating your unwavering support and credibility, for which I salute you. What I admire most about you is your ability to listen, your openness to adopting new technologies, and your unwavering dedication to your community.

You were unanimously elected to the prestigious position of President of the All India Shwetambar Samaj. Your kindness and compassion, especially toward the disabled, are truly remarkable.

You founded the Mahavir Viklang Kendra, which has helped over 15,000 beneficiaries, distributing free aid worth Rs 9 to 10 crore to date.

It is noteworthy that even at the age of 83, you remain incredibly active. You serve as a trustee of several Jain trusts, the chairman of Arihant Bank, and the leader of many other organizations.

Dr. Bangani is an affectionate, humble, and deeply religious individual. You are a firm believer in the joy of giving, a living testament to which is the Virtual Operation Theater at Mahsi Institute. You personally supported the construction of this facility, which trains Operation Theater Technicians. Dr. Prakash Bangani is a devout, knowledgeable, charitable, and humble person, with a truly great personality. I bow to this exceptional individual and feel fortunate to have you as an elder brother. I pray to God to bless you with a long and healthy life, and may you live to be a centenarian."

Dr. D.K. Taneja,
Former Dean, MGM Medical College, Indore

"Dr. Prakash Bangani is one of the most respected figures in Indore, and there are many reasons for that. After practicing in the USA for 20 years and earning a great deal of respect and recognition, he chose to return to India out of love for his parents, elder brother, and family. He is second to none when it comes to family values, and everyone knows that he has left no stone unturned in caring for his nephew, Mahendra Bangani.

He is deeply dedicated to Jain ideals and the Jain community. His entire thought process aligns with Jain teachings, with his first priority always being the Jain Guru and saints, followed by community activities.

His passion for charitable work led him to establish the renowned Arihant Hospital in the Gehen Nagar area after creating a trust.

Dr. Bangani has always been a father figure and advisor to me, especially in decisions regarding Medicare Hospital administration, where he serves on the board of directors. His thought process is clear and straightforward, providing invaluable guidance.

He is a renowned orthopedic surgeon in central India, with specialized training from the USA.
I wish him a healthy and long life."

Dr. Rajendra Lahoti,
Medicare Hospital, Indore
(Long time colleague)

"My journey as an orthopedic surgeon began in 1991 when I met Dr. Prakash Bangani, who was performing surgery at Choithram Hospital, where I was working as a registrar. As a young and inexperienced orthopedic surgeon, I was captivated, thrilled, and mesmerized by Dr. Bangani's ability to perform some of the most challenging surgical procedures with precision and perfection. His approach, which reflected the American method, was unlike anything I had seen before.

I soon began dreaming of training and working under his guidance. My mentor at the time, Dr. Vinod Naneria, played a crucial role in making this happen by speaking to Dr. Bangani on my behalf. To my great joy, Dr. Bangani agreed to take me under his wing.

Thus began my journey. Every day, I had the privilege of working alongside him, absorbing his methodical and disciplined approach to patient care. Watching him perform surgery was like witnessing Picasso paint on canvas—it was an art form. Under his mentorship, I began to evolve into the orthopedic surgeon I had always aspired to be.

Over time, he came to trust me as a sincere, disciplined, and hardworking individual with the potential to become a surgeon of substance. Sharing the surgeons' lounge in the OT complex was another invaluable learning experience, where I observed his humility and graciousness. Despite his extraordinary skills, Dr. Bangani was a humble human being, especially when interacting with colleagues.

As a young, impulsive, and short-tempered individual, I initially struggled with my emotions. However, Dr. Bangani's influence transformed me into a more tolerant, patient, and humble surgeon. He helped me develop the qualities of a true healer, and in doing so, planted the seeds of personal and professional growth within me.

In the office, I learned the most critical aspects of patient care: clinical management, assessment, planning, and surgical preparation. Dr. Bangani gave me the freedom to express my opinions on patient care, and he often praised me when I met his expectations, saying, "Pappu, I am proud of you!"

As I gained his trust and began to take on more responsibility, he would often say, "Pappu, you drive me like a slave, boy." These words filled me with pride and awe at his humility, concern, and commitment to his disciple. I couldn't have asked for more from a mentor.

Dr. Prakash Bangani is not only an accomplished orthopedic surgeon but also a great teacher, mentor, and savior of those suffering from orthopedic conditions. Beyond all these roles, he is a pure soul who has dedicated his life to transforming others with his knowledge, vision, and experience. His choice to live a simple life, almost akin to sainthood, has left a lasting impact on me.

I consider myself incredibly fortunate to have been his disciple and to have earned his faith and trust."

Dr. Praveen Agrawal
Orthopedic surgeon, CARE Hospital

"Dr. Prakash Bangani, an unparalleled personality in the medical world

History bears witness to the fact that the lives of all successful and great individuals rarely follow smooth, easy paths. They face numerous obstacles, fall, and endure hardships along rocky, uneven roads. Yet, they persist, refusing to let any obstacle deter them. Their singular purpose is to overcome challenges and, with an unwavering determination, move forward towards their goals. Dr. Prakash Bangani exemplifies this perseverance, and today, he stands as one of the most renowned orthopedic doctors in the state.

Dr. Prakash Bangani was born with natural talent. Despite not coming from a wealthy family, he has carved out a distinct identity for himself as a top doctor in the state, thanks to his unique abilities, skills, hard work, and relentless struggle. He views the medical profession as a social responsibility, often saying, "It is a gift bestowed upon me by God."

Dr. Bangani had a flourishing career as a super-specialist orthopedic and head surgeon in the USA. However, after returning to India, driven by his deep social and religious values, he was inspired to offer world-class medical services to the people of the state. This led to the establishment of Arihant Hospital and Research Center in Indore. Additionally, Dr. Bangani has played a pivotal role as the President of the Orthopedic Association of SAARC countries, further cementing his impact on the medical community.

Dr. Prakash Bangani, in addition to being a distinguished doctor, is deeply involved in religious and social work, dedicating his body, mind, and resources to the causes he believes in.

He plays an active role, both directly and indirectly, in many social institutions of the Jain Shwetambar community. With a vision of uniting various sects of Jain society, he founded the Jain Shwetambar Mahasangh, bringing the entire Shwetambar Jain community onto a single platform. He serves as the founding president of this Mahasangh.

In 1994, he established the Jain Shwetambar Academy College, followed by the creation of the Arihant Urban Co-operative Bank in 2001, which continues to flourish under his guidance. In 2018, honoring the wishes of his wife, he built the Jain Shwetambar Upashray in Race Course Road in Indore, where daily religious activities take place, including Chaturmas observances led by Guru Bhangwats.

With the blessings and inspiration of Shri Lalitprabhji and Shri Chandraprabhu Sagar Ji Maharaj Saheb, Dr. Bangani has organized numerous religious rituals and pilgrimages. He also serves as a trustee for many Jain Shwetambar pilgrimage sites and has been recognized with the prestigious Devi Ahilya Samman of Indore for his contributions.

His social and family life is an inspiration to all of us. His unwavering desire to learn something new each day, while maintaining harmony with those around him, serves as a guiding light for us to move forward. I sincerely wish for his continued health, vitality, and hope he completes 100 years of a remarkable life."

R C Mittal
Chancellor Medicaps University

Moments in time, forever captured

A family is where life begins and love never ends

Together, we laugh, we play, we love